v110717
pc: 130
ISBN Printed Book: 9781944607197
ISBN eBook: 9781944607203

TechSmith Camtasia 3 (Mac): The Essentials

"Skills and Drills" Learning

Kevin Siegel

Contents

iCONLOGiC

"Skills and Drills" Learning

About This Book

This Section Contains Information About:

- The Author, page vi
- Book Conventions, page vi
- Confidence Checks, page vii
- Project Files (Data Files), page vii
- How Software Updates Affect This Book, page viii

The Author

Kevin Siegel is the founder and president of IconLogic, Inc. He has written hundreds of step-by-step computer training books on applications such as *Adobe Captivate, Articulate Storyline, Adobe RoboHelp, Adobe Presenter, Adobe Technical Communication Suite, Adobe Dreamweaver, Adobe InDesign, Microsoft Office, Microsoft PowerPoint, QuarkXPress,* and *TechSmith Camtasia.*

Kevin spent five years in the U.S. Coast Guard as an award-winning photojournalist and has three decades' experience as a print publisher, technical writer, instructional designer, and eLearning developer. He is a certified technical trainer, a veteran classroom instructor, and a frequent speaker at trade shows and conventions.

Kevin holds multiple certifications from Adobe and CompTIA. He is also a Certified Online Training Professional (COTP) with the International Council for Certified Online Training Professionals (ICCOTP). You can reach Kevin at **ksiegel@iconlogic.com**.

Book Conventions

I believe that learners learn by doing. With that simple concept in mind, IconLogic books are created by trainers/authors with years of experience training adult learners. Before IconLogic books, our instructors rarely found a book that was perfect for a classroom setting. If the book was beautiful, odds were that the text was too small to read and hard to follow. If the text in a book was the right size, the quality of exercises left something to be desired.

Finally tiring of using inadequate materials, our instructors started teaching without any books at all. Years ago we had many students ask if the in-class instruction came from a book. If so, they said they'd buy the book. That sparked an idea. We asked students—just like you—what they wanted in a training manual. You responded, and that methodology is used in this book and every IconLogic training manual.

This book has been divided into several modules. Because each module builds on lessons learned in a previous module, I recommend that you complete each module in succession. Each module guides you through lessons step-by-step. Here is the lesson key:

❑ instructions for you to follow look like this

If you are expected to type anything or if something is important, it is set in bold type like this:

❑ type **9** into the text field

When you are asked to press a key on your keyboard, the instruction looks like this:

❑ press [**shift**]

Confidence Checks

As you move through the lessons in this book, you will come across the character at the right, which indicates a **Confidence Check**. Throughout each module, you are guided through hands-on, step-by-step exercises. But at some point you'll have to fend for yourself. That is where Confidence Checks (also known as challenges) come in. Please be sure to complete each of the challenges because some exercises build on completed Confidence Checks.

Project Files (Data Files)

During the activities that appear in this book, pretend that you work for a fictional company called **Super Simplistic Solutions**. As the lead eLearning developer, you must create all of the eLearning content for the company's products, services, and internal processes. During the lessons presented in this book, you will be using Camtasia 3 (Mac) to create eLearning content that might be accessed by learners on a desktop computer (Windows or Mac OS), a laptop, or a mobile device (such as a phone or tablet).

Your mission as you work through this book is to learn Camtasia. It's not necessary for you at this point to come up with the eLearning assets needed to create eLearning (such as videos, images, and audio files). That's where the data files come in. The data files support the lessons presented in this book and can be downloaded from the IconLogic website for free.

Student Activity: Download the Data Files

1. Download the student data files necessary to complete the lessons presented in this book.

   ❐ start a web browser
   ❐ go to the following web address: **http://www.iconlogic.com/mac**
   ❐ from the **TechSmith Camtasia** area, click **Camtasia 3: The Essentials**

   The zipped data files are typically downloaded to the **Downloads** folder on your Mac and are automatically extracted into the folder named **Camtasia3_MacData**.

2. Move the data files folder to your desktop.

   ❐ drag the **Camtasia3_MacData** folder from the **Downloads** folder to your desktop

3. You can now close the **Downloads** folder window and your web browser.

   Before starting the lessons in this book, it's a good idea to review "How Software Updates Affect This Book" on page viii.

How Software Updates Affect This Book

This book was written specifically to teach you how to use **TechSmith Camtasia (Mac) version 3**. At the time this book was written, Camtasia 3 was the latest and greatest version of Camtasia software available for the Macintosh.

With each major release of Camtasia, my intention is to write a new book to support that version and make it available within 30-60 days of the software being released by TechSmith. From time to time, TechSmith makes service releases/patches of Camtasia available for customers that fix bugs or add functionality. You can check the version of Camtasia that you are using by choosing **Camtasia 3 > About Camtasia**.

The version of Camtasia that I used while writing this book (and pulling screen captures you will see throughout the book) was **3.1.1**. I would expect TechSmith to update Camtasia with patches frequently. For all I know, the version you're using right now is 3.1.2, 3.2.1, or even newer.

I would encourage you to check for updates frequently (via **Camtasia 3 > Check for Updates**). Usually updates are minor (bug fixes) and have little or no impact on the lessons presented in this book. However, TechSmith sometimes makes significant changes to the way Camtasia looks or behaves, even with minor patches. (Such was the case when TechSmith updated Camtasia (Windows) from version 8.3 to 8.4—several features were changed, throwing readers of my books into a tizzy.)

Because it is not possible for me to recall and update printed books, some instructions you are asked to follow in this book may not perfectly match the patched/updated version of Camtasia that you might be using. If something on your screen does not match what is showing in the book, please visit the Errata page on the IconLogic website (http://www.iconlogic.com/skills-drills-workbooks/errata-pages-return-policy.html).

> **Note:** To complete the lessons in this book, you will need the Camtasia 3 software. The Camtasia software is not included in the data files you were instructed to download on the previous page. If you do not have Camtasia installed on your computer, you can purchase the software from www.techsmith.com (or download and use the free trial for a limited time).

iCONLOGiC

"Skills and Drills" Learning

Rank Your Skills

Before starting this book, complete the skills assessment on the next page.

Skills Assessment

How this assessment works

Below you will find 10 course objectives for *TechSmith Camtasia 3 (Mac): The Essentials*. **Before starting the book:** Review each objective and rank your skills using the scale next to each objective. A rank of ① means **No Confidence** in the skill. A rank of ⑤ means **Total Confidence**. After you've completed this assessment, go through the entire book. **After finishing the book:** Review each objective and rank your skills now that you've completed the book. Most people see dramatic improvements in the second assessment after completing the lessons in this book.

Before-Class Skills Assessment

1. I can add media to a project's Media Bin.	①	②	③	④	⑤
2. I can add a Quiz to a project.	①	②	③	④	⑤
3. I can add Annotations to a project.	①	②	③	④	⑤
4. I can share projects on YouTube.	①	②	③	④	⑤
5. I can record voiceover audio in Camtasia.	①	②	③	④	⑤
6. I can record screen actions using the Recorder.	①	②	③	④	⑤
7. I can add Behaviors to selected media.	①	②	③	④	⑤
8. I can add audio effects to an audio file within Camtasia.	①	②	③	④	⑤
9. I can lock a Timeline track.	①	②	③	④	⑤
10. I can add Timeline markers.	①	②	③	④	⑤

After-Class Skills Assessment

1. I can add media to a project's Media Bin.	①	②	③	④	⑤
2. I can add a Quiz to a project.	①	②	③	④	⑤
3. I can add Annotations to a project.	①	②	③	④	⑤
4. I can share projects on YouTube.	①	②	③	④	⑤
5. I can record voiceover audio in Camtasia.	①	②	③	④	⑤
6. I can record screen actions using the Recorder.	①	②	③	④	⑤
7. I can add Behaviors to selected media.	①	②	③	④	⑤
8. I can add audio effects to an audio file within Camtasia.	①	②	③	④	⑤
9. I can lock a Timeline track.	①	②	③	④	⑤
10. I can add Timeline markers.	①	②	③	④	⑤

iCONLOGiC

"Skills and Drills" Learning

Preface

In This Module You Will Learn About:

Education Through Pictures

In a previous life, I was a professional photographer. When I wasn't snapping photos during a five-year tour with the U.S. Coast Guard, I covered media events in New York City as a freelance photographer.

Just about any photographer will tell you that the goal when taking pictures is to capture a story with a few, or maybe just one, photograph. I'm betting that you have heard the saying "a picture is worth a thousand words" more than once. As a professional photographer, I lived those words.

I have spent the bulk of my career attempting to perfect the art of teaching complex concepts to busy, distracted adult learners. I have always attempted to write documentation using as few words as possible and to teach lessons as efficiently as possible.

If you are in the business of educating, you know how difficult the job of writing relevant lesson plans with fewer and fewer words can be. My step-by-step workbooks have long been known for their "skills-and-drills learning" approach. The term "skills-and-drills" learning means different things to different people. For some, it means fast-moving lessons that do not drown a person with unnecessary information. For me, "skills-and-drills learning" means learning something by doing, whatever that something is. It also means learning with a heavy dose of imagery instead of a heavy dose of text.

I learned long ago that people tend to think not with words but with pictures. Here's an example of what I mean.

> *Close your eyes for a second and picture* **three** *in your mind's eye. Open your eyes after a few seconds and read on. (See how precise I am? I know that some of you would have closed your eyes, kept them closed, and then fallen asleep without the last instruction.)*

I wasn't specific when I asked you to picture **three** was I? Because I didn't tell you how to picture *three*, it's a good bet that things such as *three cupcakes*, *three bowls of ice cream,* or *three big boxes of Cap'n Crunch* (everyone knows that the Cap'n is the best breakfast cereal *ever*) flashed into your mind's eye. Maybe a large numeral 3 appeared in your mind's eye—not the word "three." In fact, I doubt that you visualized the word *three*. Why? As I said above, people think in terms of pictures, not words. That's the reason my books usually contain hundreds of screen captures that visually explain a concept that might have taken several paragraphs to explain. And when I do have to explain a concept, I make every effort to minimize the chatter and get right to the point.

Planning eLearning Lessons

By the time you finish this workbook, you will have a better understanding of how to create technically solid eLearning lessons using Camtasia. However, that does not necessarily mean you will create *good* eLearning lessons. If you want to create good, useful lessons, plan ahead by asking yourself the following questions:

❑ **What lessons do I want to make available as eLearning lessons?** (If you are creating an eLearning course that is based on a traditional classroom course, not every lesson will be appropriate for eLearning. In addition, keep in mind that eLearning lessons aren't social events, they are completed by students who are working alone. Any lessons intended for groups may need to be removed from the course or modified to work in an online environment.)

❑ **Have I written a script?** (If you are going to capture a screen process such as the various mouse clicks performed within an application, it is critical that you document the process prior to recording anything using Camtasia Recorder.)

❑ **Do I want my projects to contain images and audio?** (Images and audio enhance the eLearning experience, but where will you find those assets? The Internet is a wonderful resource, but be careful; assets found on the Internet are rarely free and are often protected by copyright laws.)

❑ **Will there be callouts?** (Callouts are written instructions and/or descriptions that describe what is occurring onscreen. Adding callouts in the Editor is easy, but somebody will have to write and proofread them at some point. Keep in mind that while adding content to a callout is easy, Camtasia does not include a spell-check feature.)

❑ **What is the average reading level of my audience?** (Consider your audience and write content that everyone can consume. The lower the reading level of your audience, the longer it will take for learners to read the callouts. In this workbook, you will learn how to set the timing for the callouts. However, you will need to determine the appropriate pace.)

❑ **What font, font size, and colors will I use?** (Because reading text onscreen is not as easy as reading printed content, carefully consider your font choices. Verdana and Calibri are two popular font choices. A dark font color works well when you use a light background.)

When planning projects, keep in mind that the most useful projects contain the following basic elements (you will learn how to add these elements as you move through this workbook):

❑ A Title clip (telling the audience what they are going to learn)

❑ Credits and copyright clip

❑ Narration, music, and other sound effects (as appropriate)

❑ Images and animations (as appropriate)

❑ Some interactivity (such as Hotspots)

❑ An ending clip (reviewing what the audience learned)

eLearning Development Phases

The infographic below offers a visual way to think about the eLearning development process and phases. A larger version of the graphic can be downloaded from www.iconlogic.com/skills-drills-workbooks/elearning-resources.html.

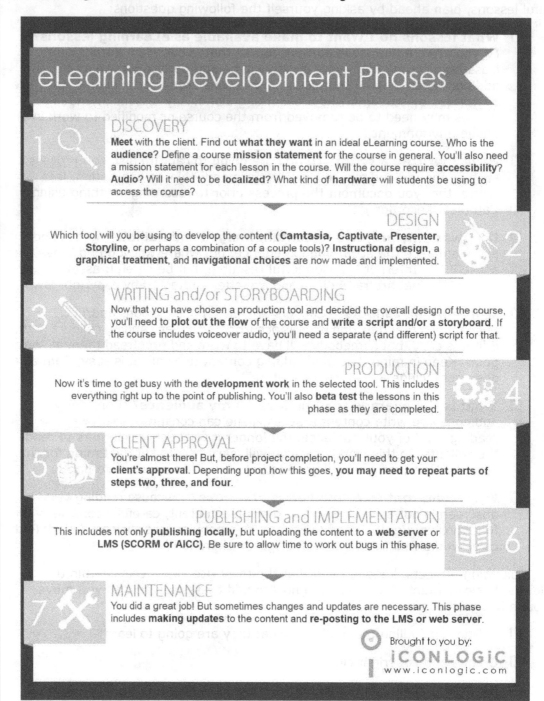

Camtasia Production Time

When I say production time, I'm referring to the actual time you will spend editing a Camtasia project. It may sound like common sense, but the longer each eLearning lesson plays, the longer it will typically take for you to produce it in Camtasia. Many new developers underestimate the number of hours needed to produce eLearning. The following table should help.

Project Size	Number of Production Hours
Small Projects (1-3 minutes of play time)	2-6 hours
Medium Projects (4-6 minutes)	8-12 hours
Long Projects (7-10 minutes)	14-20 hours
Extra-Long Projects (more than 10 minutes)	Consider splitting videos this large into smaller Camtasia projects.

Project Size and Display Resolution

When you create a new Camtasia project in the Camtasia Editor or record your computer screen using the Camtasia Recorder tool, you'll need to set either the project's width and height or the width of the recording window. For instance, you can create a project and set its size to 800 x 600 pixels. That size is perfectly fine for learners who access your content via a desktop computer with a typical monitor (typical meaning a 15-17 inch monitor).

Several years ago, monitors were small and display resolutions were low. In fact, a display resolution of 800 x 600 pixels was common. If you developed eLearning content for a display that small, a project size of 640 x 480 was ideal. A few years later, 1024 x 768 was the standard display resolution, resulting in typical eLearning lessons sized to 800 x 600.

According to **w3schools.com**, the standard desktop screen resolution today is 1366 x 768, and it's trending higher. (You'll find that available resolutions vary from system to system. For instance, I use an HP 22-inch display that doesn't support 1366 x 768. Instead, my closest options are 1360 x 768 and 1376 x 812.)

Because screen resolutions are higher than ever, many eLearning developers are seeking an optimal viewing experience for learners. But what's the ideal size for an eLearning lesson? Unfortunately, there isn't a cookie-cutter answer. The size of the lesson you create depends largely on the size of your display and its resolution. If you are recording a software simulation, the size of your project might be dependent upon the size of the software you're recording (some software cannot be resized and may take up your whole display).

There's more to consider when it comes to project size. What kind of device are your learners using? How big is their display? Is their device typically used vertically (portrait) or horizontally (landscape)? What is the typical size of an iPad? How about a Surface Pro?

If you are creating content for learners using standard desktop computers (Windows or Mac), your 800 x 600 project might look fine. However, if you upload your content to YouTube, 800 x 600 might not look right (you might see black bars on one or both sides of the video, and the video might look distorted during playback).

Selecting an ideal project size is a delicate balancing act between the size of the Camtasia capture area and your computer's screen resolution. When I use Camtasia to create recordings intended for YouTube, I set my computer's screen resolution to the manufacturer's recommendation. Then I set Camtasia's recording area to 1280 x 720. Although I could go higher with my display resolution and capture more of my screen, a higher display resolution tends to lead to smaller text that might be difficult to read.

In addition, I always use the same computer to record all of the videos used in a course. Video cards and display sizes vary from computer to computer and manufacturer to manufacturer. I want my recordings to look consistent, so I always use the same computer, same resolution, same Windows theme, and same Camtasia Recorder capture size.

Design Best Practices

Much of what you do in Camtasia will feel similar to what you can do in Microsoft PowerPoint. If you've used PowerPoint you are familiar with adding objects to a slide. In Camtasia, you add objects to the Canvas and use the Timeline to control when those objects are seen by the learner. Unlike PowerPoint, which can contain hundreds of slides, there is only one Canvas in Camtasia, and only one Timeline.

You don't have to be a seasoned designer to produce beautiful and effective Camtasia projects. Here are a few tips to get you started:

- ❏ If you're creating the content in PowerPoint, there are occasions when a bulleted list is the best way to convey an idea. Although PowerPoint uses a bulleted approach to information by default, you do not have to use that format in eLearning.

- ❏ Try splitting the bullets into separate slides with a single image to illustrate each point, or forgo the text and replace it with a chart, diagram, or other informative/interesting image.

- ❏ It is not necessary to have every bit of information you cover on the screen at one time. Encourage your audience to listen and, if necessary, take notes based on what you say, not what is shown on the screen.

- ❏ Few learners are impressed with how many moving, colorful objects each slide contains. When it comes to eLearning, the old saying, "content is King," has never been more appropriate. Ensure each of your screens contains relevant, need-to-know information and that the information is presented as clutter-free as possible.

- ❏ Consider taking more of a photographic approach to the images you use. You can easily find stock photographs on the web using any one of a number of pay-for-use websites. There are many free sites, but keep in mind that to save time and frustration (and improve on the selection and quality), you might want to set aside a budget to pay for images.

Fonts and eLearning

The most important thing about eLearning is solid content. But could you be inadvertently making your content harder to read and understand by using the wrong fonts? Is good font selection really important? Read on to discover the many surprising ways fonts can affect your content.

Some Fonts Read Better On-Screen

eCommerce Consultant Dr. Ralph F. Wilson did a study in 2001 to determine if serif fonts (fonts with little lines on the tops and bottoms of characters, such as Times New Roman) or sans serif fonts (those without lines, such as Arial) were more suited to being read on computer monitors. His study concluded that although Times New Roman is easily read in printed materials, the lower resolution of monitors (72 dots per inch (dpi) versus 180 dpi or higher) makes it much more difficult to read in digital format. Times New Roman 12 pt was pitted against Arial 12 pt, with respondents finding the sans serif Arial font more readable at a rate of two to one.

Lorem ipsum frangali puttuto rigali fortuitous confulence magficati alorem. Lorem ipsum frangali puttuto rigali fortuitous confulence magficati alorem.	Lorem ipsum frangali puttuto rigali fortuitous confulence magficati alorem. Lorem ipsum frangali puttuto rigali fortuitous confulence magficati alorem.
Times New Roman 12 pt	Arial 12 pt
520	1123
32%	68%

Source: http://www.practicalecommerce.com/articles/100159-html-email-fonts

Wilson also tested the readability of Arial versus Verdana on computer screens and found that in font sizes greater than 10 pt, Arial was more readable, whereas Verdana was more readable in font sizes 10 pt and smaller.

Some Fonts Increase Trust

A 2008 study by Sharath Sasidharan and Ganga Dhanesh for the Association of Information Systems found that typography can affect trust in eCommerce. The study found that to instill trust in online consumers, you should keep it simple: "To the extent possible, particularly for websites that need to engage in financial transactions or collect personal information from their users, the dominant typeface used to present text material should be a serif or sans serif font such as Times New Roman or Arial."

If you feel your eLearning content will be presented to a skeptical audience (or one you've never worked with before), dazzling them with fancy fonts may not be the way to go. You can use fancy fonts from time to time to break up the monotony of a dry lesson, but consider using such nonstandard fonts sparingly. Use the fancy fonts for headings or as accents but not for the bulk of your text.

The Readability of Fonts Affects Participation

A study done at the University of Michigan in 2008 on typecase in instructions found that the ease with which a font in instructional material is read can have an impact on the perceived skill level needed to complete a task.

The study found that if directions are presented in a font that is deemed more difficult to read, "the task will be viewed as being difficult, taking a long time to complete and perhaps, not even worth trying."

The results of the study by Wilson indicate that it is probably not a good idea to present eLearning material, especially to beginners, in a Times New Roman font, as it may make the information seem too difficult to process or overwhelming.

Popular eLearning Fonts

I polled my "Skills & Drills" newsletter readers and asked which fonts they tended to use in eLearning. Here is a list of the most popular fonts:

- ❑ Verdana
- ❑ Helvetica
- ❑ Arial
- ❑ Calibri

Fonts and Personas

If you are creating eLearning for business professionals, you might want to use a different font in your design than you would if you were creating eLearning for high school students. But what font would you use if you want to convey a feeling of happiness? Formality? Cuddliness?

In a study (funded by Microsoft) by A. Dawn Shaikh, Barbara S. Chaparro, and Doug Fox, the perceived personality traits of fonts were categorized. The table below shows the top three fonts for each personality objective.

	Top Three		
Stable	TNR	Arial	Cambria
Flexible	Kristen	Gigi	Rage Italic
Conformist	Courier New	TNR	Arial
Polite	Monotype Corsiva	TNR	Cambria
Mature	TNR	Courier New	Cambria
Formal	TNR	Monotype Corsiva	Georgia
Assertive	Impact	Rockwell Xbold	Georgia
Practical	Georgia	TNR	Cambria
Creative	Gigi	Kristen	Rage Italic
Happy	Kristen	Gigi	Comic Sans
Exciting	Gigi	Kristen	Rage Italic
Attractive	Monotype Corsiva	Rage Italic	Gigi
Elegant	Monotype Corsiva	Rage Italic	Gigi
Cuddly	Kristen	Gigi	Comic Sans
Feminine	Gigi	Monotype Corsiva	Kristen
Unstable	Gigi	Kristen	Rage Italic
Rigid	Impact	Courier New	Agency FB
Rebel	Gigi	Kristen	Rage Italic
Rude	Impact	Rockwell Xbold	Agency FB
Youthful	Kristen	Gigi	Comic Sans
Casual	Kristen	Comic Sans	Gigi
Passive	Kristen	Gigi	Comic Sans
Impractical	Gigi	Rage Italic	Kristen
Unimaginative	Courier New	Arial	Consolas
Sad	Impact	Courier New	Agency FB
Dull	Courier New	Consolas	Verdana
Unattractive	Impact	Courier New	Rockwell Xbold
Plain	Courier New	Impact	Rockwell Xbold
Coarse	Impact	Rockwell Xbold	Courier New
Masculine	Impact	Rockwell Xbold	Courier New

Source: http://usabilitynews.org/perception-of-fonts-perceived-personality-traits-and-uses/

iCONLOGiC

"Skills and Drills" Learning

Module 1: Exploring and Recording

In This Module You Will Learn About

- The Camtasia Interface, page 12
- The Media Bin, page 16
- The Canvas and Timeline, page 17
- Rehearsals, page 19
- Recording Screen Actions, page 22

And You Will Learn To

- Open a Camtasia Project, page 12
- Explore Camtasia Tools, page 14
- Explore the Media Bin, page 16
- Preview a Project, page 17
- Rehearse a Script, page 20
- Set Recording Options, page 22
- Select a Recording Area, page 24
- Record a Video, page 28

The Camtasia Interface

As you work through the lessons in this book, my goal is to get you comfortable with each specific Camtasia area or feature before proceeding. As with any feature-rich program, mastering Camtasia is going to be a marathon, not a sprint. Soon enough you'll be in full stride, creating awesome eLearning content using Camtasia. But before the sprint to the finish line comes the marathon itself. During these first few activities, I'd like to give you a chance to familiarize yourself with Camtasia's workspace. Specifically, you'll start Camtasia, open an existing project, and poke around Camtasia's interface a bit.

Student Activity: Open a Camtasia Project

1. Start Camtasia.

   If this is your first time starting Camtasia, a **Getting Started** project has opened by itself, and is likely playing. Do you want to get the preview to stop? Simple enough: there's a playbar just beneath the video. Click the **Pause** button on the playbar (shown in the second image below) to stop the preview dead in its tracks (audio and all).

   If this isn't your first time starting Camtasia, or you have already created some projects, I'm betting that the Getting Started project did not open at all and there is a Welcome window (shown on the next page).

   Note: If you're curious to see the Getting Started project, you can open it at any time by choosing **Help > Open Getting Started Project**. However, it is not necessary to open the Getting Started Project at all.

The **Welcome window** appears every time you start Camtasia (unless, as shown in the circle below, you deselected **Show on launch**).

Note: If you have not yet downloaded your data files, turn to the **About This Book** section at the beginning of this book and work through the **Download the Data Files** activity on page vii.

2. Open a project from the Camtasia3_MacData, Projects folder.

    ☐ if the **Welcome** window (shown above) is on your screen, click **Open Project**; if the Welcome window is not open, choose **File > Open project**

    The **Open** dialog box appears.

    ☐ navigate to **Camtasia3_MacData** folder on your computer

    ☐ open the **Projects** folder and then open Demo.cmproj

The entire screen that you see (from the **Camtasia 3** menu in the upper left of the menu bar to the objects along the bottom of the window) is known as the **Editor**.

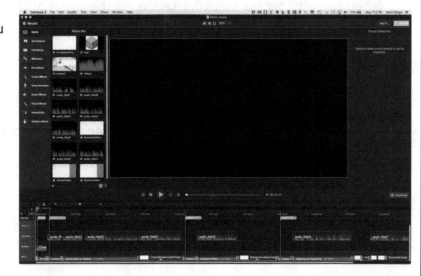

Student Activity: Explore Camtasia Tools

1. View the Voice Narration panel.

   ☐ choose **View > Tools > Voice Narration**

   The Voice Narration panel appears in the upper left of the Editor. The panel is used to record your voice (assuming you have a microphone attached to your computer). You will learn to record voiceover audio beginning on page 73.

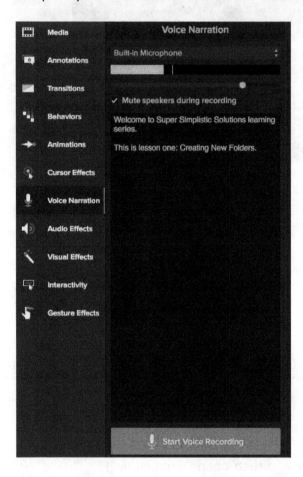

   You can also access Voice Narration via the panel at the far left of the Editor.

2. Show the Annotations panel.

   ☐ from the list of tools at the left, click **Annotations**

   There are six types of Annotations that allow you to help grab the learner's attention (including Callouts, Arrows and Lines, Shapes, Sketch, and Keystroke images). You will learn to add Annotations beginning on page 51.

3. Show the Transitions panel.

   ☐ from the list of tools at the left, click **Transitions**

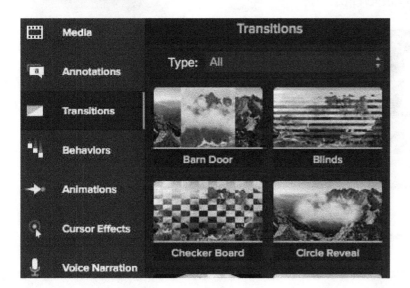

Transitions give you the ability to move from one part of your lesson to another using professional animation effects. You'll learn how to add Transitions to a project beginning on page 61.

Next you will explore the Media Bin.

The Media Bin

Every new Camtasia project has a Media Bin... but it's empty. You import assets, such as images, into the Media Bin as needed. Once assets are imported into the Media Bin, you can add them to the Camtasia Timeline.

Student Activity: Explore the Media Bin

1. View the Media Bin.

   ☐ from the list of tools at the left, click **Media**

   There are a several assets in this project's Media Bin, including videos, images, and audio clips.

   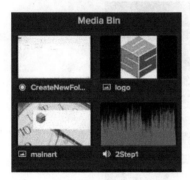

   The default view for the Media Bin is by Icons, which is nice if you like a preview of Media Bin assets. However, you may prefer List View.

2. Change the Media Bin view from Icon View to List View.

   ☐ at the bottom right of the **Media Bin,** click **List View**

3. Change the Media Bin view from Details back to Thumbnails.

   ☐ at the bottom right of the Media Bin, click **Icon View**

   You will learn how to add assets to the Media Bin beginning on page 32.

The Canvas and Timeline

The Canvas, which is in the middle of the Camtasia window, offers an excellent way to position screen elements and preview the project as you're working. As you preview a project via the Canvas, you'll be able to use the Timeline to keep track of what's happening in your project and when.

The Timeline is at the bottom of the Editor. As its name implies, the Timeline is used to control the timing of objects added to the Canvas. For instance, using the Timeline, you can force objects such as images or videos to appear at the same time, or you can force one object to appear as another goes away. You'll learn to use both the Canvas and Timeline as you move through lessons in this book. For now, you'll use the Canvas to preview the assets added to the Timeline of the demo project.

Student Activity: Preview a Project

1. Preview the project.

   ☐ on the **Canvas**, click the **Play** tool

   As the lesson plays on the Canvas, notice that a thin line and a strange-looking object move across the Timeline. The object is known as the **Playhead** (it is joined by both a green and a red rectangle, which you will learn about later). The Playhead and thin line show you where the preview is in relation to the Timeline. You will learn to work with the Timeline as you progress through the lessons in this book.

2. Detach the Canvas.

   ☐ choose **View > Canvas > Detach Canvas** (you can also find this option via the **Canvas Options** drop-down menu located just above the Canvas)

   The Canvas detaches from Editor. You can now position the panel anywhere on your display that you like. (If you have multiple monitors, you can even drag the Canvas between them.)

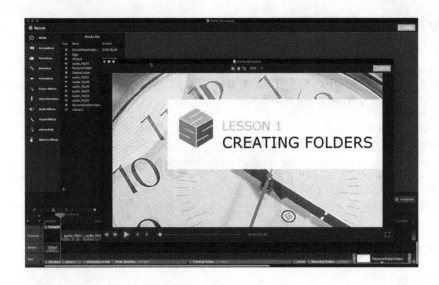

3. Explore Full Screen Mode.

   ☐ with the Canvas detached, click the **Full Screen** button (in the lower right of the Canvas)

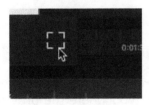

   While in Full Screen mode, you can see the lesson but not the Camtasia interface.

4. Exit Full Screen mode.

   ☐ press [**esc**] on your keyboard

5. Re-attach the Canvas.

   ☐ from the top of the detached Canvas, click the **Canvas Options** drop-down menu (shown below) and choose **Attach Canvas**

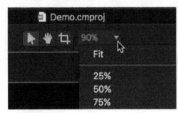

   The Canvas reattaches to the upper right of the Editor.

6. Close the project.

   ☐ choose **File > Close**

   There is no need to save any changes made to the Demo project (if prompted).

Rehearsals

You have been hired to create an eLearning course that teaches new employees at your company how to use **TextEdit** (a basic word processor that comes standard on every Macintosh). One of the lessons you plan to record using Camtasia includes how to change the page orientation within TextEdit.

Here is a sample script showing the kind of detailed, step-by-step instructions you need to create or receive from a Subject Matter Expert (SME). You are expected to perform each step written below in TextEdit.

Dear Camtasia developer, using TextEdit, record the process of changing the Page Orientation of a TextEdit document from Portrait to Landscape, and then back again (from Landscape to Portrait). Please create the recording using a capture size of 1280 x 720. Thanks. Your pal, the Subject Matter Expert.

1. Click the File menu.

2. Click the Page Setup menu item.

3. Click the Landscape orientation button.

4. Click the OK button.

5. Click the File menu.

6. Click the Page Setup menu item.

7. Click the Portrait orientation button.

8. Click the OK button.

9. Stop the recording process.

The script sounds simple. However, you will not know what kind of trouble you are going to get into unless you rehearse the script prior to recording the process with the Camtasia Recorder. Let's run a rehearsal, just as if you were a big-time movie director and you were in charge of a blockbuster movie.

Places everyone... and quiet on the set...

Student Activity: Rehearse a Script

1. Start **TextEdit** and create a **new document**.

   TextEdit can be found in the Applications folder by choosing **Go > Applications**. You can create a new document by clicking the **New Document** button (shown in the lower left of the image below) or by choosing **File > New**.

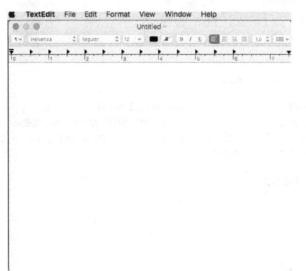

2. Rehearse the script.

   ☐ using **TextEdit** (not Camtasia), click the **File** menu

   ☐ click the **Page Setup** menu item

   ☐ from the **Orientation** area, click **Landscape**

   Note: Landscape is the **second** tool (shown below).

- ☐ click the **OK** button
- ☐ click the **File** menu
- ☐ click the **Page Setup** menu item
- ☐ click the **Portrait** orientation button
- ☐ click the **OK** button

Hey, look at that! The script worked perfectly... no surprises. You are now ready to click through the exact steps again. Only this time, you will record every click that you make using the Camtasia Recorder. During the recording process, Camtasia will create a video of the process.

3. Leave TextEdit running and return to Camtasia.

Recording Screen Actions

When you record screen actions using Camtasia, you should pretend you are using a video recorder and creating a movie (you're both the director and the producer). During the recording process, everything you do is recorded exactly as you do it. Every delay, every good click, bad click, double-click... everything is recorded. If you move your mouse too fast and race through a series of steps, the resulting video will play back the cursor speed in real time. Move too slowly, and your learners will tear their collective hair out as they watch the cursor slowly move across the screen.

In the steps that follow, you'll select a recording area and then record the process of changing the Page Orientation in Notepad.

Student Activity: Set Recording Options

1. Change Camtasia's Preferences so that you are prompted to save after every recording.

   ❏ from within **Camtasia 3**, choose **Camtasia 3 > Preferences**

   The General dialog box opens.

   ❏ click **Recording**

   ❏ from the **After recording** area, choose **Prompt to Save**

   With the **Prompt to Save** option selected, you will be prompted to name the video when you are finished recording and select a Save destination.

After recording:	Prompt to Save	⬍

2. Change the Preferences so that recordings are not automatically deleted.

   ❏ from the **Save recordings to** area, remove the check mark from **Delete after**

Save recordings to:	/Users/i
☐ Delete after	14 days

   With **Delete after** disabled, older recordings won't be automatically deleted by Camtasia.

The remaining Recording options should match the image below.

Recording

General Recording Timeline Canvas

Capture Frame Rate: Full-motion (30 fps)

System Audio: Install component

☑ Show countdown before recording
☑ Show menu bar icon

After recording: Prompt to Save

Recording Name Prefix

⦿ Default ("Rec ")

◯ Custom

Save recordings to: /Users/iconlogic/Movies/Camtasia 3

☐ Delete after 14 days Change... Reveal

In my opinion, the two most important default Preferences that you did not change are **Capture Frame Rate** and **Show countdown before recording**.

By default, recordings are captured at 30 frames-per-second (fps). The higher the frame rate, the smoother a recorded video will be. However, when captured at a high frame rate, the file size of a video can be huge (especially if you record for more than a few minutes). If you find that your videos are excessive, you can experiment with lowering the frame rate here prior to recording (which will lower the size of your recording, but could also lower the quality of the video).

Having the **Show countdown** option turned on is a good default. Without this option enabled, the recording process will begin the instant you click the Start Recording button... so fast you'll possibly find yourself unprepared and make mistakes while recording.

❑ close the Recording dialog box

Student Activity: Select a Recording Area

1. Start the Camtasia Recorder.

   ☐ from within Camtasia, choose **File > New Recording**

   The Camtasia Recorder opens and there is a large green box that is likely surrounding your entire display. The green box is known as the Recording area. You will next change the Recording area's size and select a specific area.

2. Set a recording size and select a recording area.

   ☐ on the **Camtasia Recorder**, click the **first drop-down menu** at the left (shown circled in the image above) and choose **720 HD (1280x720)**

   The recording area is now a green, dashed line. You can now specify any area of your screen as the Recording Area. In this instance, the Recording Area you need is the TextEdit application (its menu bar and application window).

   Note: If you have a small screen, 1280x720 may be too large of a recording area. You can manually resize the capture area to any size that works best (via a corner resize handle like the one shown below).

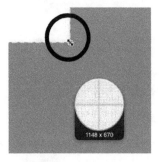

❏ drag the **middle** of the Recording Area so that the upper left of the area begins in the TextEdit menu bar similar to the image below

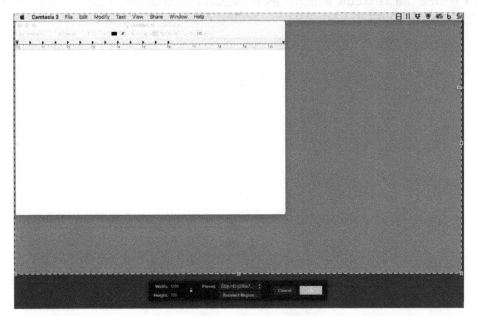

Note: You might find the step above a bit clunky because there is no visual drag area anywhere in the Recording Area. However, dragging the middle of the entire area does allow you to reposition the Recording Area without resizing it. When repositioning the Recording Area, note the appearance of your mouse cursor. You're looking for a hand icon as shown below (indicating that you are moving the Recording Area, not resizing it).

❏ click the **OK** button

3. Ensure the TextEdit window size and the Recording Area match.

   ❑ resize the TextEdit window as necessary so that the TextEdit window fits nicely within the Camtasia Recording Area

4. Disable the Camtasia Recorder camera and microphone.

   ❑ on the Camtasia Recorder, deselect both the camera and microphone (if the options are gray, you don't have either a camera or a microphone connected to your computer)

I'm a fan of including voiceover audio in eLearning. In my experience, voiceover audio almost always enhances the learner experience. The dilemma you might face is whether you should record the audio and the video at the same time or add the audio to the video later.

If you are creating micro-learning (very short videos used as "just-in-time learning"), you might want the more informal, natural feel of audio narration recorded while you click through a software process. On the other hand, if you are creating a longer, more formal course, you may want a more formal sound. In this case, I would encourage you to either hire professional talent or record your own voice in a studio and with high-quality equipment.

You can easily create your audio narration either way with Camtasia. With some practice, you can record your voice with the Camtasia Recorder while you're creating the video. Or you can record your voice in the Camtasia Editor while you are producing the video. (You will learn how to record and edit audio in Camtasia beginning on page 67). You can also record your voice separately, using any number of audio editing tools (such as Audacity, Sound Forge, or Adobe Audition) and import the audio files into the Camtasia Media Bin.

What about capturing yourself with your video camera? I'm not a fan of that. Ask yourself this question: "Is it really necessary to insert myself into this lesson?" The answer will likely be no. If you do elect to record yourself, are you sure you're dressed appropriately? Yes? Okay, but what about what's behind you? Is there a poster in the background that's inappropriate? If you look good and the background is great, what about the lighting around you? What about your camera angle? Because there's much to consider when it comes to self-videos, consider not doing them. Besides, if you have awesome existing videos of yourself, you can insert them into Camtasia later (see page 32).

But enough about all that. Let's go ahead and record your first software demonstration.

Student Activity: Record a Video

1. Record a software demonstration.

   ☐ on the Camtasia Recorder, click the red **Start Recording** button

   You'll see a three-second countdown.

   ☐ before the counter gets to zero, position your mouse pointer in the center of the Notepad window

   After the counter disappears, your every move (and the time it takes you to move) is being recorded.

   ☐ moving steadily (not too fast), move your mouse pointer to the **File** menu

   ☐ click the **Page Setup** menu item

   ☐ from the **Orientation** area, click **Landscape**

   ☐ click the **OK** button

   ☐ click the **File** menu

   ☐ click the **Page Setup** menu item

   ☐ click the **Portrait** orientation button

   ☐ click the **OK** button

2. Stop the recording process.

   ☐ press [**command**] [**option**] [**2**] on your keyboard

   Once you press the Stop recording hotkeys on your keyboard, the recording process terminates and you are prompted to save the recording.

   ☐ navigate to **Camtasia3_MacData > Video_Files**

   ☐ name the recording **Change Page Orientation**

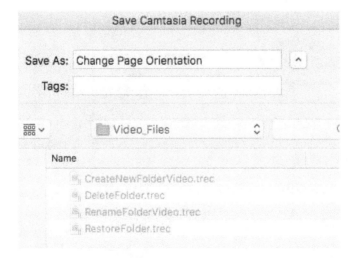

   ☐ click the **Save** button

3. Close the Camtasia Recorder.

---

4. Import a recording into a new Camtasia project.

   ☐ from within Camtasia, choose **File > New Project**

   ☐ from the **left side** of the Camtasia window, click **Media** (to open the Media Bin)

   ☐ on the **Media Bin**, click **Import Media**

   ☐ navigate to **Camtasia3_MacData > Video_Files**

This is where you should have saved the video you just recorded. In addition to your video, there are other videos that support upcoming modules in this book. Notice that the videos have a **trec** extension which is a TechSmith proprietary format. These **trec** video files can be imported into the Camtasia Editor and used to produce eLearning content. However, **trec** files cannot be shared, opened, or used by other media players.

   ☐ select **Change Page Orientation.trec**

   ☐ click the **Import** button

The asset appears on the Media Bin.

5. Add a video to the Timeline and preview the video.

   ☐ on the **Media Bin**, right-click the video you just imported and choose **Add to Timeline at Playhead** (if your mouse does not support right-clicking, you can press [**control**] on your keyboard and **click** your mouse to see **Add to Timeline at Playhead**)

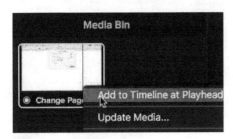

The video is added to a track on the Timeline. And notice that the Canvas now includes a preview of your recording.

☐ on the **Canvas**, click the **Play** tool

If you are unhappy with your first recording, the good news is that it's free to create more. All you'd need to do is click the **Record** tool in the upper left of the Camtasia window or choose **File > New Recording**.

6. Close the Camtasia project (there is no need to save it).

Recording Confidence Check

1. Record a new software demonstration of anything you'd like to record on your computer. (For instance, use your web browser to add a Favorite; change the appearance of text in your word processor of choice, or edit the appearance of an image in your favorite image editor.)

2. When finished recording, save the recording to **Camtasia3_MacData > Video_Files** with any name you like.

3. In Camtasia, create a new project and import your new video to the Media Bin.

4. Add the new Media Bin asset to the Timeline and then preview the video.

5. Close the Camtasia project (there is no need to save it).

iCONLOGiC

"Skills and Drills" Learning

Module 2: Adding Media

In This Module You Will Learn About:

- Videos, page 32
- Images, page 36
- Multi-Track Projects, page 38
- Cursor Effects, page 43

And You Will Learn To:

- Import a Video, page 32
- Import Images, page 36
- Add a Track, page 38
- Create a Watermark, page 41
- Add Cursor Effects, page 43

Videos

During the first module of this book, you were introduced to the tools that make up Camtasia, opened a Camtasia project, and explored the Editor interface (page 12). Then you used the Camtasia Recorder to record screen actions (page 28). Now you'll create a project from scratch using the Camtasia Editor.

The first thing you will learn to add to the new project is video. When it comes to importing video files, you can import any of the following video formats:

- ❑ **trec** (a recording created with newer versions of the Camtasia Recorder, which you learned how to use on page 28)

- ❑ **camrec** (a recording created with older versions of the Camtasia Recorder)

- ❑ **mp4** or **mpeg** (a file format created by the Moving Picture Experts Group, which was designed to compress video into a digital format)

- ❑ **avi** (Audio Video Interleave, an early Microsoft video file format)

- ❑ **wmv** (Windows Media Video developed by Microsoft)

- ❑ **mov** (Apple's proprietary format that plays using Apple's "Quick Time" player).

Student Activity: Import a Video

1. Ensure that Camtasia is running. If there are open projects, you can close them (there is no need to save).

2. Create a new project.

   - ❑ on the Welcome window (via the Help menu), click the **New Project** button or choose **File > New Project**

3. Set the project dimensions.

   - ❑ from the top of the Canvas, click the drop-down menu and choose **Project Settings**

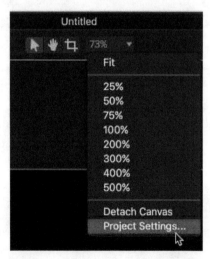

The Project Settings dialog box opens. You can control such project attributes as the color of the background (currently it's black by default), and the width and height. The videos that you're going to be importing were recorded at 1280x720 (just like the video you recorded in TextEdit). While you can change the dimensions of the Canvas at any time, for now working with a video and Canvas that are the same size is going to work well.

☐ from the **Dimensions** drop-down menu, choose **720p HD 1280x720**

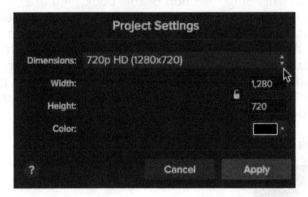

☐ click the **Apply** button

4. Import a video.

☐ from the top left of the **Editor**, click **Media** to display the **Media Bin**

☐ on the **Media Bin**, click **Import Media**

The Open dialog box appears. Any supported video file you can access from your computer can be imported using this dialog box.

☐ from **Camtasia3_MacData > Video_Files** folder, open **CreateNewFolderVideo**

The video appears in the Media Bin.

5. Add a video to the Timeline and Preview.

   ❑ on the **Media Bin**, right-click (or [**control**] click) the video you just imported and choose **Add to Timeline at Playhead**

   The imported video is added to the Timeline and appears on the Canvas. As first mentioned in the "About This Book" section of this book, you are pretending that you work for an awesome fictional company called **Super Simplistic Solutions**. Your job is to build a series of short eLearning courses that teach basic computer skills to people who work for the company. One of those courses is how to work with computer folders (how to create them, rename them, and delete them). The video you imported demonstrates the process of creating a folder on a Windows-based computer, which is what most employees use at Super Simplistic Solutions.

   ❑ on the **Canvas**, click the **Play** tool

   The video demonstrates how to create a new folder on a computer.

6. Save the project.

   ❑ choose **File > Save**

   ❑ name the project **CreateNewFolder** (ensure you are saving to **Camtasia3_MacData** > **Projects**) and then click the **Save** button

7. On the **title bar** of the Camtasia Editor, notice that the saved project has a **cmproj** extension.

   If I were going to give you a pop quiz right about now, a couple of questions you might come across would be about extensions for Camtasia assets. During the past few modules, you have learned that videos created with the Camtasia Recorder have a **trec** extension; and you've learned that Camtasia projects have a **cmproj** extension. Got it? (There's no quiz coming up by the way, so breathe easy.)

Video Confidence Check

1. Ensure that the **CreateNewFolder** project is open.

2. On the **Timeline**, right-click (or [**control**] click) the video you just added and choose **Delete**.

   The video is removed from the Timeline. Now that it has been removed from the Timeline, it would no longer appear in a produced lesson. However, notice that the video remains in the Media Bin. Items in the Media Bin remain available for you to preview and add to the Timeline, but items in the Media Bin will not appear in a produced video unless they have been added to the Timeline.

3. Ensure the **Playhead** is positioned as far left of the Timeline as it will go.

4. Right-click (or [**control**] click) the video in the Media Bin and choose **Add to Timeline at Playhead** to add the video to the Timeline again.

5. On the Timeline, zoom closer to the video in Track 1 by clicking the **Zoom timeline in** tool.

   The ability to Zoom closer to Timeline objects will prove useful later when you need to split the audio or synchronize the video with other Timeline objects. You can always use the **Zoom timeline out** tool to move farther away from the Timeline or drag the slider (the circle between the plus and minus signs).

   Clicking the magnifying glass icon (shown below), brings your entire Timeline into view.

6. Save the project (choose **File > Save Project** or press [**cmd**] [**s**] on your keyboard).

7. Close the project.

Images

Few things enhance an eLearning lesson better than quality images. Camtasia supports many of the standard graphic formats, including bitmaps, GIFs, and JPEGs. You can learn about the different graphic formats with a quick Internet search (one site that I find helpful is **Dan's Data** (www.dansdata.com/graphics.htm). If you don't have ready access to photographs and other images, I've had great success with BigStockPhoto.com and StockPhoto.com. Both of these sites offer awesome collections of inexpensive, royalty-free images. You'll also find some wonderful eLearning assets on the eLearning Brothers website (www.elearningbrothers.com).

Student Activity: Import Images

1. Open an existing Camtasia project.

   ☐ choose **File > Open project**

   ☐ open **Camtasia3_MacData > Projects > ImageMe.cmproj**

   This project is identical to the one you were just working on. It has the CreateNewFolderVideo in the Media Bin and on the Timeline.

2. Import an image to the Media Bin.

   ☐ choose **File > Import > Media**

   ☐ from the **Camtasia3_MacData** folder, open the **Image_Files** folder

   ☐ open **logo.png**

   The logo image appears in the Media Bin.

3. Import another image.

   ☐ choose **File > Import > Media**

   ☐ from the **Image_Files** folder, open **mainart.jpg**

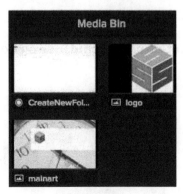

Timeline Confidence Check

1. On the Timeline, drag the **CreateNewFolder** video to the **right** approximately one-half inch (this leaves space to the left of the video for the mainart image).

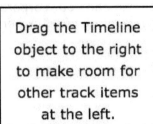 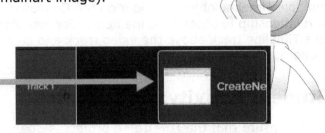

> Drag the Timeline object to the right to make room for other track items at the left.

2. Drag the **mainart.jpg** image from the Media Bin to the beginning of Track 1 on the Timeline.

3. On the Timeline, drag the **CreateNewFolder** object **left** until it just bumps up against the mainart image).

4. On the **Canvas**, click the **Play** button to preview the project.

   Notice that the mainart image appears on the Canvas and then, after a few seconds, the image disappears and the video showing how to create a new folder plays.

   If you want to have one Timeline object appear, then disappear, and then another Timeline object appear, all you have to do is add objects to the Timeline horizontally and move them (or stretch them) on the Timeline to control when they appear and for how long. However, if you want to have multiple Timeline items appear at one time, you'll need multiple Timeline tracks... something you'll learn about next.

5. Save your work.

Multi-Track Projects

You've added two assets to the Timeline (the video and the mainart image). Both objects appear on a single Track called Track 1. You can easily add additional tracks to the Timeline. Once you have multiple tracks, you can precisely control when multiple Timeline objects appear on the Canvas and how items appear on the Canvas in relationship to other Timeline items. For instance, you can add your corporate logo to a Timeline track above the video track and create a watermark effect... perfect for corporate branding.

Student Activity: Add a Track

1. Ensure that the **ImageMe** project is open.

2. Insert a new track.

   ☐ on the top left of the Timeline, click **Add a track**

   On the Timeline, notice that **Track 2** has been added above Track 1. Because Track 2 is above Track 1 on the Timeline, anything you add to Track 2 will be layered in front of anything on Track 1 when viewed on the Canvas.

   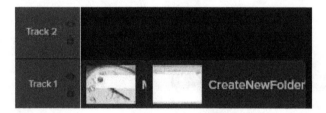

3. Add an image to Track 2.

   ☐ if necessary, drag the Playhead left to the beginning of the Timeline

   ☐ on the Media Bin, right-click (or [**control**] click) **logo.png** and choose **Add to Timeline at Playhead**

   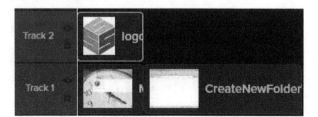

Only one object can be positioned on a track at a particular time point on the Timeline. Because the Playhead is positioned at 0.00 time and there is an object on Track 1 at that time point, the logo is automatically added to the next available track (in this instance, the beginning of Track 2). If you hadn't manually added the second track prior to adding the image to the Timeline, the track would have been added automatically.

4. Ensure Timeline Snapping is enabled.

    ❐ choose **View > Enable Timeline Snapping** (if necessary, ensure the menu item has a check next to it)

5. Change when the logo appears on the Timeline.

    ❐ on **Track 2**, position your mouse pointer in the **middle** of the **logo**

    ❐ on the **Timeline**, drag the logo **right** until its **left edge** lines up with the left edge of the CreateNewFolder video on Track 1

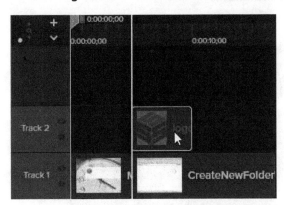

6. Position the Playhead and preview a portion of the video.

    ❐ on the **Timeline**, double-click the CreateNewFolder **video** object

    The Playhead, which indicates the current frame selected (or point in time) on the Timeline, should now be positioned just before the CreateNewFolder video.

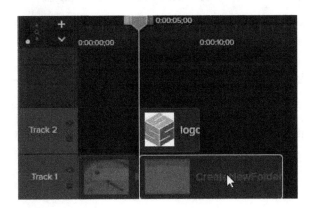

    ❐ on the **Canvas**, click **Play**

    The logo image appears in the middle of the Canvas by default. In addition, the logo disappears long before the video is finished.

7. Extend the play time for the logo.

☐ on the **Timeline**, use your mouse to point to the **right edge** of the logo object

Note: If you are very close to the Timeline, it might be helpful to zoom out a bit before working with the Timeline objects.

☐ when your mouse pointer changes to a **double-headed arrow**, drag the **right** edge of the logo object **right** until the logo's bar ends when the video ends (as shown in the images below)

8. Preview the timing changes.

☐ on the Timeline, double-click the **CreateNewFolder** video object

Double-clicking the Timeline object moves the Playhead to just before the **CreateNewFolder** video on the Timeline.

☐ on the **Canvas**, click the **Play** button to preview the project

On the Canvas, notice that the logo image sticks around for the duration of the video. (It's too big, and it doesn't work all that well in the middle of the video... but you'll fix those issues next.)

9. Save your work.

Student Activity: Create a Watermark

1. Ensure that the **ImageMe** project is open.

2. Display the Properties panel.

   ☐ on Track 2, double-click the **logo** to move the Playhead to the beginning of the logo on the Timeline

   ☐ right-click (or [**control**] click) the **logo** and choose **Show Properties** (if you see **Hide Properties** instead, you can move to the next step)

   At the **right side** of the Editor, notice that there is a **Properties** panel.

3. Make the logo smaller.

   ☐ on the **Properties** panel, drag the **Scale** slider **left** to change the Scale to **50%** (if you find it difficult to get to exactly 50, type **50** into the Scale field at the right)

4. Lower the Opacity of the logo.

   ☐ on the Properties panel, drag the **Opacity** slider **left** to change the Opacity to **40%** (again, if you find it difficult to get to exactly 40, type **40** into the field at the right)

   The lower the Opacity, the more see-through the logo becomes.

5. Change the object's video position.

☐ on the Canvas, drag the logo near the bottom right of the background

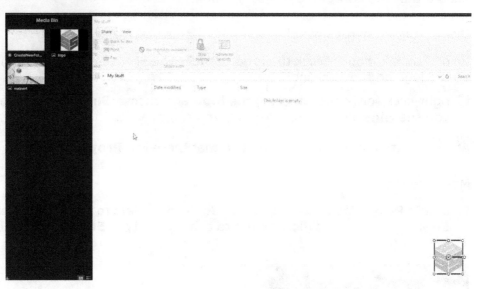

6. Save your work.

Cursor Effects

Earlier in this module you added a video to the project that demonstrates the process of creating a new folder on a computer (page 32). You've previewed that video several times during this module, so it's likely that you have already noticed that in the video the mouse, through the process of creating a new folder, moves from one part of the window to the next. As the cursor moves, there are no click sounds or visual effects to draw the learner's attention to the clicks. Unfortunately, you're working with an existing video, so there's no way to alter the cursor's behavior... or is there? Because the video was created with the Camtasia Recorder, and it's a **trec** file, the cursor can be modified in the Editor (you can easily add such enhancements as click effects and click sounds).

The ability to alter the cursor properties in the Camtasia Editor is an exclusive feature available only in **trec** and **camrec** videos created by the Camtasia Recorder. If you import any other type of video into the Editor (such as an **mp4** video), you cannot modify the cursor properties.

Student Activity: Add Cursor Effects

1. Open an existing project.

   ❑ choose **File > Open project**

   ❑ open **Camtasia3_MacData > Projects > MouseMe.cmproj**

2. Preview the lesson.

   ❑ on the **Timeline**, double-click the **CreateNewFolder** video to move the Playhead to the beginning of the video

   ❑ on the **Canvas**, click the **Play** button to preview the project

   As the video plays, pay particular attention to the mouse cursor. It's moving around the screen just fine, but you can't hear any mouse clicks. During the steps that follow, you'll add both a click sound and a visual effect.

3. Add a Left Click effect to the cursor.

   ❑ on the **Timeline**, double-click the **CreateNewFolder** object to move the Playhead to the beginning of the video (and select the video on the Timeline)

   ❑ from the list of tools at the left, click **Cursor Effects**

The Cursor Effects panel opens. Using this panel, you can add visual effects to the mouse throughout the video.

❏ from the top of the Cursor Effects panel, select **Cursor Effects**

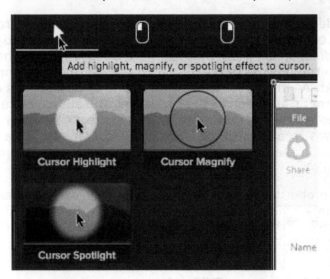

❏ right-click (or [**control**] click) **Cursor Highlight** and choose **Add to Selected Media**

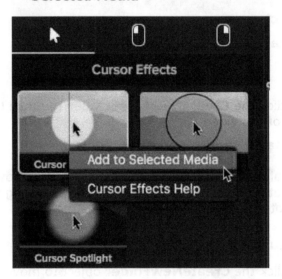

The effect is instantly added to the selected video. On the Timeline, you can tell an effect has been added to media via the **Show effects** arrow beneath the media.

4. Preview the video.

   ❏ on the **Canvas**, click the **Play** button to preview the video

   You've just added a nifty highlight effect to the mouse. *How cool is that?*

   Note: You can control the appearance of the effect (such as the Opacity) via the **Properties** panel at the right of the Canvas. In the image below, I changed the Opacity of my highlight to 30%, making it easier to see the text behind the highlight.

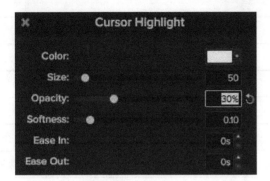

Cursor Effects Confidence Check

1. On the Timeline, click **Show effects** just below the video.

2. Right-click (or [**control**] click) the Cursor Highlight effect and choose **Remove Effect**.

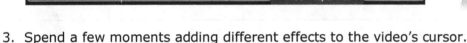

3. Spend a few moments adding different effects to the video's cursor.

   Note: Experiment with the **Left Click** effects on the Cursor Effects panel (including the Left Click Sound).

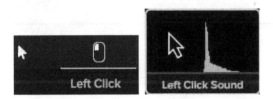

   Note: If you select to add a Click Sound, check out the Sound and Volume control available on the Properties panel.

4. Preview the video to see/hear your new cursor effects.

5. When finished, save your work and close the project.

Notes

iCONLOGiC
"Skills and Drills" Learning

Module 3: Groups, Annotations, and Animation

In This Module You Will Learn About:

And You Will Learn To:

Groups

As you add media to the Camtasia Timeline things are likely to get a bit, shall we say, frenzied. You can have several Timeline tracks, and each track can contain multiple items. Because you can use the Timeline to precisely control how long each item appears on screen, changing the timing of one object can easily foul up its relationship to objects on other tracks. Given how complex Timeline relationships can become, you'll appreciate Camtasia's ability to group objects. Rather than moving an individual object on the Timeline (only to realize you left a related object on a different track behind), you can group objects and move everything in the group at one time.

Student Activity: Create a Group

1. Open **AnnotateMe.cmproj** from the **Camtasia3_MacData > Projects** folder.

2. Extend the Duration of an image.

   ☐ on the **Timeline**, right-click (or [**control**] click) the **mainart** object (the first object in Track 1) and choose **Duration**

   A Duration panel appears.

   ☐ change the **Duration** to **20** seconds and press [**enter**]

   The mainart image on the Timeline stretches and pushes the CreateNewFolder video right. Because it is located in a different track, the logo you are using as a watermark on the video does not move.

   If things stay as they are, it looks like you will have to potentially move multiple objects every time you change an object's timing. This is a perfect use-case for grouping. In the next step, you'll group the CreateNewFolder video and the logo. Once the objects are grouped, timing changes made to objects left of the group push the group right.

3. Undo the last step.

   ☐ choose **Edit > Undo** (or press [**cmd**] [**z**])

   The timing for the mainart image should be back to 5 seconds.

---

4. Create a group.

☐ on the **Timeline**, click in the space above Track 2 (to ensure that no Timeline objects are selected)

☐ on the **Timeline**, select the **CreateNewFolder** video in Track 1

☐ press [**shift**] and select the **logo** in Track 2 (then release [**shift**])

Both the video and the logo should now be selected.

☐ right-click (or [**control**] click) either of the selected objects and choose **Group**

The objects have now been grouped. The logo, which was in Track 2, has been moved into the new group on Track 1.

5. Name a group.

☐ right-click (or [**control**] click) the new group and choose **Rename Group**

The group's default name, Group 1, is selected.

☐ change the group's name to **Creating Folders** and press [**enter**]

6. Extend the Duration of the mainart image again.

☐ on the **Timeline**, right-click (or [**control**] click) the **mainart** object (the first object in Track 1) and choose **Duration**

☐ change the **Duration** to **30** seconds and press [**enter**]

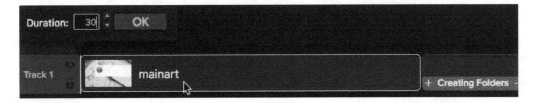

This time the entire group moves right on the Track to accommodate the extended playtime of the image.

7. Remove an empty track.

☐ at the left of the Timeline, right-click (or [**control**] click) the words **Track 2** and choose **Remove Track**

8. Save your work.

Note: To ungroup objects, right-click (or [**control**] click) a group and choose **Ungroup**. If you'd like to see the objects that make up a group, click the **plus sign** in the upper left of a group to expand the group. Once you've opened a group, you can close a group by clicking the **X** shown in the image below.

Annotations

Annotations are typically used to explain a concept being shown on screen or to highlight something. There are several types of Annotations, including Callouts (shapes that can contain text), Arrows, Lines, Shapes, Motions, and Keystroke Callouts. In the Demo project you opened at the beginning of this book, there are several Callouts synchronized with the voiceover audio. One of the Callouts from that project is shown in the image below (the words CREATE and FOLDERS). During the activities that follow, you will add and then format a few Callouts.

Student Activity: Add a Callout

1. Ensure that the **AnnotateMe.cmproj** project is open.

2. Insert a Callout.

   ☐ on the **Timeline**, double-click the **mainart** image to move the Playhead to the far left of the Timeline

   ☐ from the list of tools at the left (the **Tools** panel), click **Annotations**

   The Annotations panel opens.

   ☐ on the **Annotations** panel, click **Callouts** (the first Annotation type)

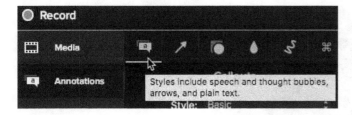

   ☐ from the **Style** drop-down menu area, choose **Basic**

   ☐ right-click (or [**control**] click) the **white rectangle with the black text** and choose **Add to Timeline at Playhead**

3. Format the Callout's text.

    ☐ with the **Callout** selected on the **Canvas**, open the **Properties** panel (if necessary)

    ☐ at the top of the **Properties** panel, click **Text Properties**

    ☐ from the **Font** drop-down menu, change the Font to **Verdana**

    ☐ from the menu to the right of the **Font** menu, click the **Choose any color** drop-down menu

    ☐ change the text color to **Black**

    ☐ change the **Alignment** to **Left**

4. Remove the Callout's border.

    ☐ ensure that the **Callout** is still selected

    ☐ at the top of the **Properties** panel, click **Annotation Properties**

    ☐ change the line **Thickness** to **0**

    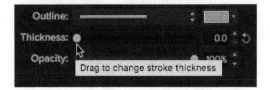

5. Remove the Callout's Drop Shadow.

   ❏ ensure that the Callout is still selected

   ❏ at the top of the **Properties** panel, click **Visual Properties**

   ❏ click the **X** to the left of Drop Shadow

6. Add the Callout text.

   ❏ replace the existing text in the Callout with the words **CREATE FOLDERS**

   ❏ resize and position the Callout on the Canvas similar to the image below

7. Change the caption's font size.

   ❏ **highlight all of the text** within the Callout

   ❏ at the top of the Properties panel, click **Text Properties**

   ❏ change the font size to **80**

8. Save your work.

Student Activity: Apply Image Color to Callout Text

1. Ensure that the **AnnotateMe.cmproj** project is open.

2. Pick up color from an image and apply it to selected text.

   ❑ in the callout, **highlight** the word **CREATE**

   ❑ at the top of the **Properties** panel, click **Text Properties**

   ❑ from the color area, select the **Select color from image** tool

   ❑ using the **Select color from image** tool, click the green "S" on the logo

   The color you clicked with the **Select color from image** tool is applied to the highlighted text in the Callout.

3. Save your work.

Callouts Confidence Check

1. Click in front of the word **FOLDERS** and press [**enter**].

2. Press [spacebar] a few times to indent the word **FOLDERS**.

3. On the Timeline, right-click (or [**control**] click) the Callout and **Copy** it to the clipboard.

4. On the Timeline, position the Playhead just to the right of the Callout.

5. **Right-click** (or [**control**] click) on the Timeline just to the right of the existing Callout and choose **Paste Media At Playhead**.

Because you positioned the Playhead prior to pasting, the pasted Callout is pasted after the existing Callout on Track 2.

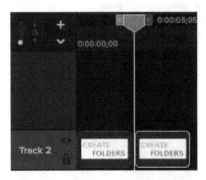

6. On the Canvas, double-click the new Callout and change the word **CREATE** to **RENAME**.

7. On the Timeline, position the Playhead just to the right of the second Callout and then **Paste Media At Playhead**.

8. Double-click the new Callout and change the word **CREATE** to **DELETE**.

9. Change the word **FOLDERS** to **RESTORE**.

10. Save your work.

11. Close the project.

12. Create a **new** Camtasia project.

13. Spend a few moments adding some of the other Annotations to the project. (There is no need to save the project, so play as much as you'd like.)

14. As you explore the Annotations, resize and move the objects around the Canvas.

15. Check out the **rotation** handle just to the right of center on all Canvas objects. Play around with how it works by dragging the handle (shown in the star shape below).

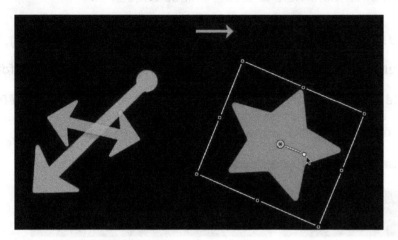

16. As you rotate, check out how you can also change Rotation values on the Properties panel via Visual Properties.

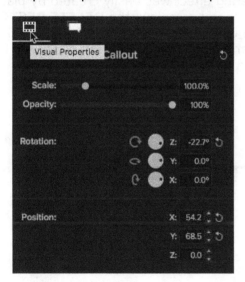

17. Did you play with the Sketch Motions? If you add them to the project and then preview (via the Play control on the Canvas playbar), you'll see them in action.

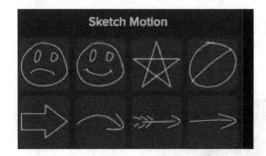

18. When finished exploring the Annotations, close the project without saving.

Behaviors

Behaviors, also known as Effects, are animations that are typically used to add some visual excitement to your project. Behaviors can be attached to images, video clips, and several types of Annotations. A Behavior can be added to a single object or stacked together with other Behaviors to create unique effects.

Student Activity: Add a Behavior to a Callout

1. Open **BehaveMe.cmproj** from the **Camtasia3_MacData > Projects** folder.

    The BehaveMe project is similar to the AnnotateMe project you closed a few moments ago except it has some additional Callouts added to Tracks 2 and 3. In particular, notice the three ampersands (**&**) added to Track 2.

    The layering order is important. Notice that each ampersand is **behind** the Callouts you added earlier. This layering effect was easily created by placing the ampersand in a lower track. In the image below, the **DELETE RESTORE** Callout is in Track 3; the ampersand is in Track 2. Objects in higher tracks are positioned in front of objects in lower tracks. In addition, the opacity of the Callouts was set to 0 (via the Properties panel, Annotation Properties).

    In the next step, you'll be adding a Behavior to the ampersands.

2. Add a Behavior to a Callout.

    ☐ on Track 2, double-click the first **ampersand** to highlight it on the Canvas

    ☐ from the list of tools at the left, click **Behaviors**

    ☐ right-click (or [**control**] click) **Jump And Fall** and choose **Add to selected Media**

The Jump and Fall effect is added to the Callout and appears below the Timeline object. It can be removed by right-clicking (or [**control**] clicking) and choosing **Remove Effect**.

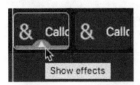

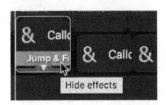

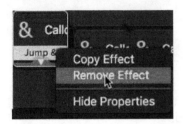

3. Preview the effect.

   ☐ with the Playhead positioned just to the left of the **ampersand** you just altered, click the **Play** button on the Canvas

   The ampersand drops in from the top of the canvas, bounces a few times, and then drops off the bottom of the Canvas.

4. Change the effect's timing.

   ☐ on the **Timeline**, drag the **left edge** of the **ampersand** Callout **right** a few seconds

5. Preview the timing change.

   ☐ with the Playhead positioned just to the left of the **RENAME FOLDERS** Callout (the second Callout on Track 2), click the **Play** button on the Canvas

   This time the Callout appears and then, a few seconds later, the animated ampersand does its thing.

6. Modify the effect.

   ❏ on Track 2, double-click the **ampersand** you've been working with to highlight it on the Canvas

   Currently, the ampersand drops in from the top of the Canvas. Let's see what other tricks you can make the Callout perform.

   ❏ on the **Properties** panel, select the **In** tab

   ❏ from the **Style** drop-down menu, choose **Hinge**

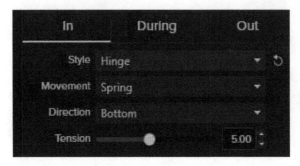

7. Preview the effect.

   ❏ with the Playhead positioned just to the left of the **ampersand** you just altered, click the **Play** button on the Canvas

   This time the ampersand swings up from the bottom of the Canvas.

Behaviors Confidence Check

1. Spend a few moments playing with the **In**, **During**, and **Out** settings available on the **Properties** panel.

2. Add a Behavior to the remaining two ampersands (remember, there are ampersands at Timeline positions 11;05 and 16;05).

3. Preview the effects and adjust the timing of the ampersand Callouts as you see fit.

4. Using the Properties panel, adjust the effects as you see fit.

5. Select and then group mainart image and the Callouts (name the group **Introduction to Folders**).

6. Save your work.

Transitions

You can use Transitions to add a smooth, professional visual break between clips in a project. There are several Transition types available on the Transitions panel, including Glow, Fold, and, my personal favorite, Cube rotate.

Student Activity: Add a Transition to a Group

1. Open **TransitionMe.cmproj** from the **Camtasia3_MacData > Projects** folder.

   This project picks up where you left off during the last Confidence Check except I've added a few more grouped assets to the Timeline (Get Ready and Lesson 1).

2. Preview a few Transitions.

   ❒ from the panel at the left, click **Transitions**

   ❒ from the list of **Transitions**, hover above **Fade**

   A sample of the Fade Transition appears on the transition.

   ❒ on the **Transitions** panel, hover above the **Wheel** Transition to see a preview

   ❒ on the Transitions panel, hover above the **Cube rotate** Transition to see a preview

3. Add a Transition to selected media.

   ❒ on the **Timeline**, select the **Get Ready** group

   ❒ on the **Transitions** panel, right-click (or [**control**] click) the **Cube rotate** Transition and choose **Add to Selected Media**

   On the Timeline, a transition has been added to the beginning of the selected group... and it's been added to the beginning of the next group. You can tell that a transition has been added via the green rectangles. The transition was added to the second group (even though you didn't select that group) because, by default, transitions are added to the beginning and end of a selected group and to the beginning of the next group that it is touching.

4. Save your work.

Student Activity: Modify Transition Timing

1. Ensure that the **TransitionMe.cmproj** project is open.

2. Preview the video from the beginning.

   As the video plays on the Canvas, the Cube rotate transition should appear at the beginning and end of the first clip and again at the beginning of the second clip. It's a cool effect, but you'd like to speed it up a bit.

3. Modify Transition Timing.

   ❏ on the Timeline, select the first green transition icon and drag it a bit to the **left** (this will speed it up)

4. Preview the video.

   The timing for the first transition should be a bit faster than before.

Transitions Confidence Check

1. Working in the **TransitionMe** project, add any Transitions you like to each of the groups.

2. Preview the project to see transitions.

3. Save your work.

4. Close the project.

Scaling

Camtasia's Scaling feature is useful if the width and height of your recorded video is larger than the size of your Canvas and you want to focus the learner's attention on a specific area of the screen. By applying SmartFocus, learners will automatically be moved closer to the screen. Adding SmartFocus is as simple as positioning the Playhead where you want to add the effect, accessing the SmartFocus feature (via Animations), and stretching and/or moving the SmartFocus window.

Student Activity: Add a Scale Up Animation

1. Create a new project.

   ❑ choose **File > New Project**

   By default, the Canvas size is **1920x1080**. You're going to make it much smaller.

2. Resize the project.

   ❑ at the top of the Canvas, click the drop-down menu and choose **Project Settings**

   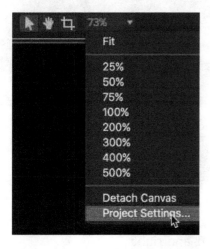

   ❑ from the **Dimensions** drop-down menu, choose **480p SD (854x480)**

   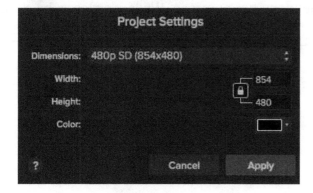

   ❑ click the **Apply** button

3. Add the following videos to the Media Bin: **CreateNewFolder** and **RenameFolder** (Need help? You learned how to import videos on page 32).

4. Add the **CreateNewFolder** video to the beginning of the Timeline.

   On the Canvas, notice that the video shrinks down to fill the screen. However, at this reduced project size, it's very difficult to see what's happening onscreen.

5. Add a **Scale Up** animation to the video.

   ❏ on the **Timeline**, position the Playhead at the point in the video where the cursor is just about to click the **Home** tab (approximately **3:26**)

   ❏ from the tools at the left, click **Animations**

   ❏ drag the **Scale Up** animation onto the Timeline

6. Preview the animation.

   ❏ on the **Timeline**, drag the Playhead left and right

   On the **Canvas**, notice that the Scale Up works but the zooming occurs in the middle of the video, not the menu bar onscreen. While it's nice to be closer to the action, you'll need to pan (move) the video a bit so learners can see the cursor moving to the Home tab.

7. Pan an animation.

   ☐ on the **Timeline**, select the **larger circle** on the **Scale Up** animation you just added to the video (the circle to the right of the arrow)

   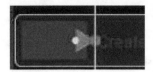

   The larger circle is a visual indicator of the end of the animation effect.

   ☐ on the Canvas, drag the video **down and to the right** until you can see the upper left of the video (the cursor over the Home tab on the Ribbon)

   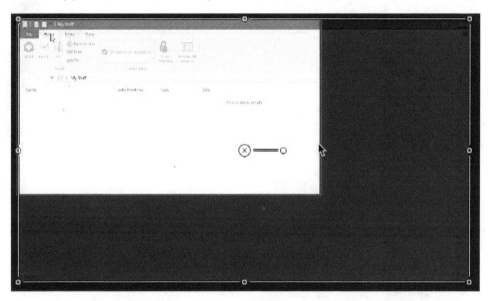

8. On the Timeline, drag the Playhead left and right again.

   You're closer to the screen and the action on the Home tab. However, you'd like to get even closer to the action.

9. Change the Scale percentage.

   ☐ on the **Timeline**, select the **larger circle** on the Scale Up animation

   ☐ on the Properties panel, change the Scale to **125**

   ☐ on the **Canvas**, drag the video **down and to the right** again until you can see the upper left of the video (the cursor over the Home tab on the Ribbon)

10. On the Timeline, drag the Playhead left and right again.

    You're now a bit closer to the action.

Scaling Confidence Check

1. Position the Playhead near the end of the video and add the **Scale to Fit** animation.

2. Add the RenameFolder video to the Timeline after the existing video.

3. Spend a few moments experimenting with the **Scale Up**, **Scale Down**, and **Scale To Fit** animation.

4. When finished exploring, close the project (there is no need to save it).

iCONLOGiC

"Skills and Drills" Learning

Module 4: Audio

In This Module You Will Learn About:

And You Will Learn To:

Importing Audio Media

When you import audio media into a Camtasia project, the following formats can be imported: WAV, MP3, M4A, and WMA.

WAV (WAVE): WAV files are one of the original digital audio standards. These kinds of files, while of extremely high quality, can be very large. In fact, typical WAV audio files can easily take up to several megabytes of storage per minute of playing time. If you have a slow Internet connection, download times for files that large are unacceptable.

MP3 (MPEG Audio Layer III): MP3 files are compressed digital audio files. File sizes in this format are typically 90 percent smaller than WAV files.

M4A: M4A (MPEG 4 Audio): M4A files are similar to MP3 files. They are smaller than WAV files but of excellent quality and could one day replace MP3s.

WMA (Windows Media Audio): WMA is a popular audio format developed by Microsoft. WMA files are often smaller than MP3 files.

Student Activity: Add Background Music to a Video

1. Open **AudioMe.cmproj** from the **Camtasia3_MacData > Projects** folder.

2. Add an audio file to the Media Bin.

   ❑ choose **File > Import > Media**

   ❑ navigate to the **Audio_Files** folder within the **Camtasia3_MacData** folder

   ❑ open **2Step1.mp3**

   The imported audio clip appears in the Media Bin.

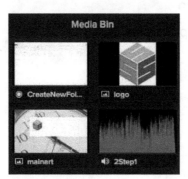

3. Add the imported audio to a track on the Timeline.

   ❑ on the Media Bin, right-click (or [**control**] click) **2Step1.mp3** and choose **Add to Timeline at Playhead**

   The audio file appears on the Timeline in Track 2 as a series of sharp lines—a waveform.

Audio Confidence Check

1. Still working in the **AudioMe** project, notice that the music lasts longer than the video.

2. On the Timeline, **Track 2**, drag the right edge of the 2Step1.mp3 audio clip left until the audio ends when the video ends at 59;02 seconds.

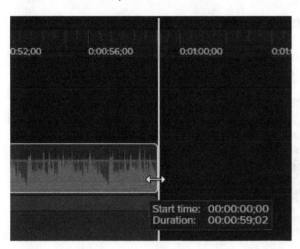

3. Preview the video again. The audio ends when the video ends. However, the audio cuts off a bit too abruptly. You will take care of that next when you learn to fade specific areas of the background music in and out.

Student Activity: Fade Audio In and Out

1. Ensure that the **AudioMe** project is open.

2. Preview the video to hear the background audio you just added to the Timeline. Notice that the audio starts right away and is at full volume.

3. Fade audio in.

   ☐ from the panel at the left, click **Audio Effects**

   Note: If your display is small, you may need to click **More** at the bottom of the Tools panel to see **Audio Effects**.

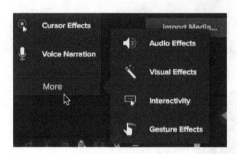

   ☐ on the **Timeline**, select the background music on Track 2

   ☐ from the **Audio Effects** panel, right-click (or [**control**] click) **Fade In** and choose **Add to Selected Media**

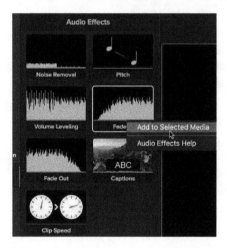

   Notice that a ramp has been added to the left of the waveform.

   The ramp begins at the left of the waveform and then gets taller until the audio hits a consistent level. You can manually drag the green line to control how the audio fades in, but you'll probably be happy with the level established automatically by Camtasia.

Fading Confidence Check

1. Preview the entire video to hear the fade effect you added to the audio.

2. At the left of Track 2, select and then drag the large dot toward the right a bit to increase the amount of time the Fade In will be in effect.

3. Preview the beginning of the video. You should hear that the Fade In effect lasts longer than before.

4. At the end of the video, notice that the audio already fades out (it was set to fade out by the person who provided the audio file). However, you'd like to further control the fade.

5. Add the **Fade Out** effect to the background music.

6. Go to the end of the Timeline and drag the dot left to increase the amount of time the Fade Out will be in effect.

7. Preview the end of the video. You should hear that the Fade Out effect lasts longer than before.

8. Spend a few moments experimenting with the audio fade timing until the effects sound good to you.

9. Save your work.

10. Close the project.

Voice Narration

Camtasia allows you to record your own narration and sound effects and add them to any available Audio Track. If you plan to record your own audio, you will first need a microphone connected to your computer. After the microphone, consider the following:

Voiceover Scripts: You saw an example of an eLearning script on page 19. In addition to a step-by-step eLearning script, it's important to include a voiceover script for yourself or your voiceover talent... and rehearse the script as much as possible prior to recording. Rehearsals are the perfect opportunity to find which words in the script, if any, are going to trip up you or the narrator.

Location, Location, Location: Get yourself into a quiet space—consider a "Do Not Disturb" sign on your door. You might be surprised by how much noise there is in an average office. Your microphone will probably pick up every nearby sound. Before using your office or cubicle as your recording studio, take a break and listen. Turn down the ringer volume on your phone. Is the water dripping? Is the printer squeaking? Is your neighbor coughing nonstop?

Audio Setup: If you plan to use high-end audio hardware, such as a mixer or preamplifier, plug your microphone into the hardware and then plug the hardware into your computer's "line in" port. Set the volume on your mixer or preamplifier to just under zero (this will minimize distortion).

Microphone Placement: The microphone should be positioned four to six inches from your mouth to reduce the chance that nearby sounds will be recorded. Ideally, you should position the microphone above your nose and pointed down at your mouth. Also, if you position the microphone just to the side of your mouth, you can soften the sound of the letters S and P.

Microphone Technique: It's a good idea to keep a glass of water close and, just before recording, take a drink. To eliminate breathing and lip-smack sounds, turn away from the microphone, take a deep breath, exhale, take another deep breath, open your mouth, turn back toward the microphone, and start speaking. Speak slowly. When recording for the first time, many people race through the content. Take your time.

Monitor Your Audio Level As You Record: When recording your audio, you will see an Input Level meter on Camtasia's Voice Narration panel indicating how well the recording process is going. When the meter is green to yellow, you're fine. However, when the meter is orange to red, you are being warned that you are too close to the microphone or that you are speaking too loudly.

Student Activity: Record Voice Narration

1. Using a word processor, open **CreatingFoldersVoiceoverScript** from the **Other_Assets** folder within the Camtasia3_MacData folder.

   Let's pretend for a moment that you've been hired to serve as the voiceover talent for an eLearning project. It's quite possible you'd get a script similar to the file you've just opened.

   Audio File 1:
   Welcome to Super Simplistic Solutions learning series.
   This is lesson one: Creating New Folders.

   Audio File 2:
   This lesson is going to teach you how to create a new folder on your computer, how to rename it, and how to both delete and restore recycled items.

   Audio File 3:
   When creating folders keep in mind that you can create as many folders as you need.

   ---

2. Rehearse the audio script.

   ☐ using a slow, deliberate cadence, read the following out loud:

   Welcome to Super Simplistic Solutions learning series.

   This is lesson one: Creating New Folders.

   Next you'll record your voice in Camtasia. (You can close the script if you'd like.)

3. Using Camtasia, open **NarrateMe.cmproj** from the **Camtasia3_MacData > Projects** folder.

4. Record voiceover audio.

   ☐ on the **Timeline**, position the Playhead at the beginning of the **Lesson 1** group

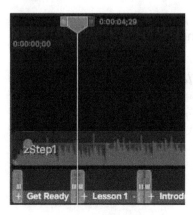

☐ from the panel at the left, click **Voice Narration**

On the Voice Narration panel, notice that I have already pasted the part of the voiceover script you'll be recording. Alternatively, you can print the script and have it beside you during the recording phase.

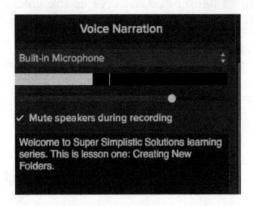

☐ from the top of the Voice Narration panel, select **your microphone** from the drop-down menu

☐ ensure **Mute speakers during recording** is selected

Muting the speakers is a good idea for this video because you have background audio in Track 2. If you don't mute the audio, it will likely play through your computer speakers and ruin your voiceover audio.

And now... prepare yourself! Once you start the recording process, there isn't a count-down or any kind of warning. Instead, Camtasia simply records your voice. While you are recording, the video will play on the Canvas so you can see what's happening in your lesson while you narrate.

☐ click the **Start Voice Recording** button

☐ using a slow, deliberate cadence, read the following out loud:

Welcome to Super Simplistic Solutions learning series.

This is lesson one: Creating New Folders.

5. When finished, click the **Stop** button.

   The audio file is automatically saved to the Media Bin and added to the Timeline.

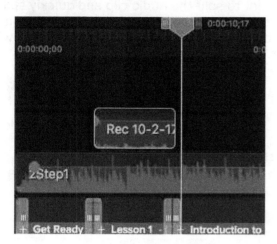

6. Preview the video.

   You should be able to hear your new voiceover audio. However, you should also be concerned that the audio is hard to understand with the background music playing so loudly. You'll fix that shortly.

7. Save your work.

8. Close the project.

Splitting Media

You will find Camtasia's ability to split segments on the Timeline to be a valuable feature. Have you imported an audio clip that's too long and difficult to manage? Click at the top of Timeline where you want to split the audio clip and quickly split the clip into as many segments as you need. Want to add a transition in the middle of a video clip? Because transitions cannot be inserted in the middle of a clip, click where you need a transition and insert a split.

Student Activity: Split a Music Clip

1. Open **SplitMe.cmproj** from the **Camtasia3_MacData > Projects** folder.

   This is basically the same project you were just working on except the voiceover audio that you recorded and inserted during the last activity has been replaced by professional voiceover audio.

2. Preview the video.

   Notice that the background music and voiceover audio are fighting with each other. In fact, the background music is so distracting, it's tough to tell what the narrator is saying.

   In the steps that follow, you will split the background music into two parts and then manipulate the two audio pieces on the Timeline so that they don't fight with the voiceover audio. During the splitting process, it's possible not only to split the background music but also to inadvertently split media in other tracks. To prevent that you'll need to lock the tracks. To that end, you will lock both tracks 3 and 1. Changes you make to the media in Track 2 (which will remain unlocked) will not accidentally affect media in other tracks.

   When I first learned how to use Camtasia, there were no books to buy and there was little professional training available. Because I am self-taught on how to use the tool, I was never educated about the need to lock certain tracks before editing objects on other tracks. If I highlighted part of a track and deleted a selection, the same selection in unlocked tracks would also be deleted! In one project, I learned my mistake only hours later when previewing the finished video. By then, it was far too late to undo my mistake.

3. Lock Tracks.

   ☐ at the far left of the Timeline, click the padlock to the left of **Track 1** and **Track 3** to **lock** those tracks (only **Track 2** should remain unlocked)

4. Split the background music in Track 2 into two segments.

   ☐ on the top of the Timeline, click at the **4;29** mark to position the Playhead

   ☐ on the Timeline, select the audio in **Track 2**

   ☐ right-click (or [**control**] click) the **Playhead** and choose **Split**

And just like that, the background music has been split into two segments.

Audio Timing Confidence Check

1. Select the second segment of the background music.

2. Drag the **left edge** of the segment to the right until it lines up with the end of the **audio_file01** media in **Track 3**.

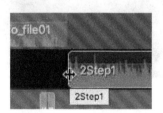

3. Select the **first segment of the background music** and, using the **Audio Effects** panel, **Fade Out** the media.

4. Select the second segment of the background music and **Fade In** the media.

5. Preview the video.

   The background music stops pretty much when the narrator begins to speak. Nice. The music shouldn't start again until after the narrator is finished speaking.

   There's a problem now with the timing for Lesson 1 group. The group isn't on the Canvas long enough to match the voiceover audio. To fix that, you'll need to change the timing of a few Timeline objects.

6. On the Timeline, unlock both locked tracks.

7. Press [**Cmd**] and, on the Timeline, select both the **Introduction to Folders** and **Creating Folders** groups.

8. Release the [**Cmd**] key and drag both selected groups to the **right** to align with the end of **audio_file01** and the beginning of **2Step1**.

9. Stretch the **Lesson 1** group right to make its playtime match the voiceover audio in Track 3.

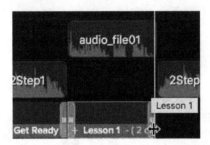

   Your tracks should now look like this.

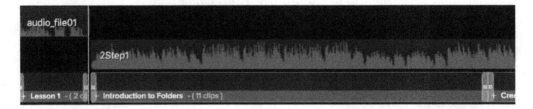

10. Save your work.

11. Close the project.

Audio Editing

Earlier in this module you learned how to edit an audio clip by fading the volume in and out. Camtasia offers you other editing options such as the ability to cut segments of a waveform and even replace unwanted audio with silence.

Student Activity: Rename Tracks

1. Open **EditMyAudio.cmproj** from the **Camtasia3_MacData > Projects** folder.

   This project is similar to the project you were just working on with a few notable exceptions. First, two of the tracks have names that are more descriptive than Track 1, Track 2, etc. (Voiceover and Background Audio).

   There's also additional voiceover audio in the Voiceover track.

2. Rename a track.

   ☐ on the far left of the **Timeline**, double-click the name **Track 1**

   ☐ replace the text with the word **Main** and press [**enter**]

   Naming your tracks is always optional. However, in larger projects with more than just a few tracks, I find this practice makes it easier and more efficient to produce my projects.

Student Activity: Silence and Cut Audio

1. Ensure that the **EditMyAudio** project is open.

2. Preview an audio clip.

   ☐ on the **Timeline**, position the Playhead to the left of the **audio_file02_silence** media and preview the video

   There are two strange sounds in the clip and there's a bit of dead air at the end of the audio file. You have two choices for removing unwanted audio segments: delete the content or replace the content with **Silence**. When deleting, the duration of the audio clip is reduced by the amount of audio that is deleted. However, if your goal is to simply remove a problem in the audio clip (such as click sounds) without altering the duration of the clip, using Silence is an ideal solution.

3. Replace a selection of audio with Silence.

   ☐ lock the **Background** and **Main** tracks

   As you learned earlier, locking a track ensures changes made to unlocked tracks will not affect locked tracks.

   ☐ on the **Voiceover** track, double-click **audio_file02_silence** to position the Playhead at the beginning of media

   ☐ at the top of the **Timeline**, drag the **Zoom** slider **right** to zoom closer to the Timeline

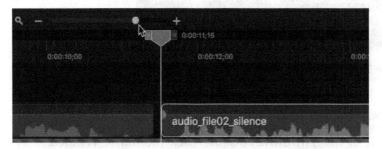

At this enhanced view, you can get a better look at the waveform that makes up the audio file. You can see that the narrator's audio levels are consistent across the wave.

Take a look at about the **15.15 second** mark on the Timeline. There's a spike in the wave that isn't consistent with the rest of the wave. This part of the wave is an erroneous sound that you need to edit.

❒ drag the Playhead to the beginning of the errant sound

❒ drag the Playhead's red out point right to highlight the sound

❒ press [**spacebar**] to play just the selected sound

❒ right-click (or [**control**] click) the selection and choose **Silence Audio**

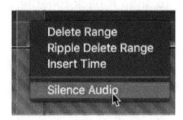

The click sound or whatever it was has been removed without altering the playtime of the media.

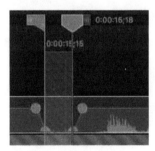

❒ double-click the Playhead to deselect the segment and snap the Playhead back together

Audio Editing Confidence Check

1. There's another errant sound at the 16.23 second mark on the Timeline.

2. Select and then replace the sound with Silence.

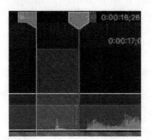

   Note: Remember to double-click the Playhead to snap it back together.

3. Save your work.

4. Close the project.

iCONLOGiC

"Skills and Drills" Learning

Module 5: Sharing, Extending, and Quizzing

In This Module You Will Learn About:

And You Will Learn To:

Sharing Videos

Sharing is the process of taking your final work and rendering a version of the project that can be accessed without the need for the learner to own Camtasia. Shared output files are not the original Camtasia project files, so the learner cannot modify the content. Instead, learners are able to view your output (assuming they have access to it) using free tools such as Web browsers or media players. (Media players are included on most computers out of the box.)

Camtasia's Share menu contains myriad menu items that allow you to quickly publish a project as a standalone file that you can email to a colleague or customer. The standalone file can be opened by free media players such as Windows Media Player or Apple's QuickTime Player. Once you have shared a project from within Camtasia, you can then uploaded the shared content to your corporate server or Learning Management System (LMS). Your content can be used by learners on devices such as desktop computers, laptops, and mobile devices (smart-phones, tablets, etc.). There are even Share options allowing you to render and then automatically upload your content to Screencast.com, YouTube, or Google Drive (assuming you have existing accounts on those websites).

Student Activity: Share an MP4

1. Open **ShareMe.cmproj** from the **Camtasia3_MacData > Projects** folder.

2. Produce the project as a standalone video file.

   ☐ choose **Share > Local File**

   The Export As dialog box opens.

   ☐ change the **Export As** name to **Create_Folders_MP4_Only**

   ☐ navigate to the **Produced_Videos** folder (the folder is inside **Camtasia3_MacData** folder)

Export As:	Create_Folders_MP4_Only	^
Tags:		

🎛 ⌄	📁 Produced_Videos	⌄	

   ☐ from the **File format** drop-down menu at the bottom of the dialog box, choose **Export to MP4 (.mp4)**

   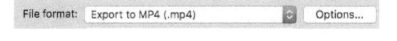

   ☐ click the **Export** button

The project is exported (rendered) and you'll be able to track its progress during the process via the dialog box shown below. At this point, you won't be able to work within Camtasia without first canceling the export process.

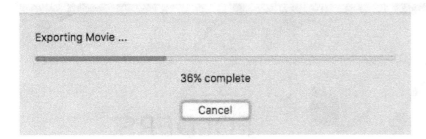

Once the export is complete, you'll see an Export finished dialog box.

❒ click the **Reveal in Finder** button

The Produced Videos folder opens. The only file in the folder at this point is the single video that you just exported.

3. Open the video file in a media player.

❒ right-click (or [**control**] click) the video and choose **Open With > QuickTime Player.app**

The published video opens.

☐ click the **Play** button on the playbar to start the video

I don't know about you, but I think this whole production process went just a bit too smoothly. I bet you're thinking that I set this project up in advance so that when you produced it things would go perfectly. And I'm betting that you're betting that once you try to do this on your own, the wheel's going to come off the cart and nothing is going to work as smoothly as it just did.

Let me assure you that the production process you just worked through was based on default settings you'll find in Camtasia "out of the box." There was nothing in the ShareMe video set up in advance to ensure success in the Sharing process. In fact, you can run through the production process using any Camtasia project and your result should match those shown in this activity.

You will get a chance to play with some of the other Sharing options in a bit. For now, enjoy your progress. Believe it or not, you are now a published eLearning author. Congratulations!

4. Close the media player and return to the Camtasia project.

Student Activity: Share to YouTube

1. Ensure that the **ShareMe** project is open.

2. Share a video to YouTube.

   ❑ choose **Share > YouTube**

   If you have not already done so, you'll be required to Sign in to your YouTube account.

   ❑ if necessary, click the **Sign in** button

3. Give the video a Title, Tags (keywords), and a Description.

   ❑ in the Title field, type **Creating New Folders**

   ❑ in the Tags field, type **training, windows, file management**

   The tags make it easier for YouTube users to search YouTube and find your video.

   ❑ in the Description field, type **This demonstration will teach you how to create a folder using Windows.**

4. Set the Privacy level.

   ❑ from the **Privacy** drop-down menu, choose **Private**

5. Render the video.

   ☐ click the **Share** button

   The video is exported again. However, once finished this time, it is automatically posted to YouTube.

   ☐ from the Share History screen, you can view your posted video by clicking the **Visit** button.

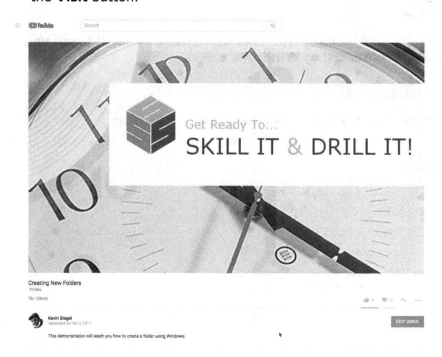

6. If you visited YouTube, you can close the browser and, back in Camtasia, close the Share History screen.

Student Activity: Export as a Web Page

1. Ensure that the **ShareMe** project is open.

2. Share the video so it will play via a Web browser.

   ☐ choose **Share > Local File**

   ☐ change the **Export as** name to **ShareMe_Web_Version**

   ☐ if necessary, navigate to the **Produced_Videos** folder

   ☐ from the **File format** drop-down menu at the bottom of the dialog box, choose **Export to MP4 (.mp4)**

   ☐ select **Export as Web Page**

   ☐ click the **Export** button

   ☐ click the **Reveal in Finder** button

   The first time you shared a file (earlier in this module), you shared the file as a video. And once it was generated, the process yielded a single file. This time, you've created assets that will rely on each other to correctly open in a browser. Should you upload these assets to your web server, the files must be kept together.

   ☐ open the **ShareMe_Web_Version** folder

   There's single html file in the folder (this is the start page for the lesson) and a media folder.

Name		Date Modified
⚙ index.html		Today, 1:38 PM
▶ 📁 media		Today, 1:38 PM

   ☐ double-click **index.html** to open the page in your default browser

   ☐ click the **Play** button in the middle of the screen to play the lesson

3. When finished, close the browser window to close the lesson.

4. Return to the Camtasia project.

Sharing Confidence Check

1. If you have a **Google Drive** account, Share your project to your drive. (You should be able to use the same account credentials you used for sharing on YouTube.)

   If you work with a team of Camtasia developers who use Camtasia for Windows, it's likely that you will be asked to share your project with others (so they can modify the project). Sharing projects between developers is not the same as using the Share menu so you can render content for your learner. Sharing a project sounds simple enough: copy the **cmproj** file to a shared drive such as Dropbox or a network drive and that's that. However, assets added to the Media Bin are **linked** to their original location. When you import media into Camtasia from a local or network drive and then send the Camtasia project file to someone outside your network, that person is prompted to locate the linked media before the project opens in his/her copy of Camtasia. It's likely that that person will not be able to find those linked assets.

   Here's how to get past that problem:

2. Choose **File > Export for Windows**.

3. Save the Zip As **ForMyWindowsFriends** and ensure you're saving to the **Produced_Videos** folder.

   The resulting zip file contains all of your project's assets. You can now share this zip file with fellow Camtasia developers who will have everything they need to open and edit the project (assuming they also have Camtasia 3 (Mac), or version 9 (Windows) installed).

4. Close the project.

Extending Frames

If you record screen actions and then import audio later (as you've done several times during the lessons in this book), synchronizing the screen actions shown in the video with the voiceover audio can be difficult. In those instances where the voiceover audio is referring to something before the event occurs in the video, you'll be happy to learn that you can extend the playtime of a single video frame until the video and the audio catch up to each other.

Student Activity: Extend a Video Frame

1. Open **ExtendMe.cmproj** from the **Camtasia3_MacData > Projects** folder.

2. At the **2:26;00 second mark** on the Timeline, notice that **audio_file07** has been added to the Timeline above the **RestoreFolder** video.

3. Position the Playhead at **2:26;00** and **preview** the video.

   The narrator is talking about the Recycle Bin and how much its appearance has changed. However, the video is just a bit ahead of the voiceover audio. Rather than re-record the video, you're going to freeze the video just long enough for the voiceover audio and video to be synchronized.

4. Lock the **Voiceover** and **Background** tracks.

5. Split a video into two segments.

   ❑ on the **Timeline**, zoom a bit closer to the **2:26;00** mark

   ❑ on the **Timeline**, drag the **Playhead** a bit right to **2:26;16**

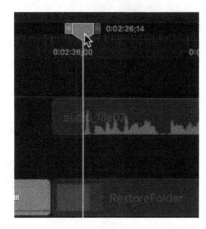

   This is the point in the video just before the cursor moves toward the Recycle Bin.

   ❑ on the **Timeline**, select the **RestoreFolder** media

   ❑ right-click (or [**control**] click) the **Playhead** and choose **Split**

   The video has been split into two segments.

   ❑ drag the **Playhead** right to **2:29;05**

❏ drag the larger of the two video segments **right** until it snaps at the Playhead's position (at **2:29;05**)

The gap between the two video segments (shown in the image above) is going to be filled with the first segment's last frame.

❏ leave the **Playhead** positioned at **2:29;05**

❏ select the first part of the split video (the smaller segment)

❏ choose **Edit > Playhead > Extend Frame to Playhead**

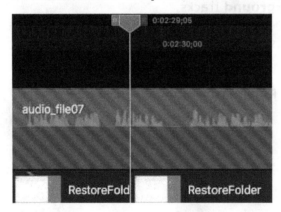

6. Preview the video from the beginning of the first RestoreFolder segment.

   Extending the frame has slowed down the video just enough that the screen actions and voiceover audio are pretty well synchronized.

7. Save your work.

8. Close the project.

Quizzes

I have never been a very good test-taker. The minute I hear a course I am taking includes a quiz, I fixate on the pending quiz or exam and get myself so stressed out that I stop learning.

It's only recently that I've come to understand quizzes and exams for what they are... an opportunity to learn. Had I thought of quizzes as just another part of the learning process, perhaps I wouldn't have stressed myself out so much and would have performed better on tests (there have been many poor performances over the years).

Many people compare eLearning to live training. It's not a fair comparison because eLearning lacks live, human interaction. In a live, instructor-led class, an experienced trainer can gauge the effectiveness of a lesson by asking the learner a question about something taught in the class. When a trainer asks questions, the learner has an opportunity to share what was learned, and prove lesson comprehension. It's perfectly fine for the learner in a live class to get a question wrong. In that instance, the trainer gives the correct answer and learning has taken place. In my classes, I typically ask direct and overhead questions of my students. If the answer given is wrong, I give the correct answer. Later, I'll ask that same learner the question again... only I reword the question (I'm sneaky like that). In almost every instance, the learner answers the rephrased question correctly.

Although an eLearning lesson cannot provide trainer-to-learner interaction, you can still engage the learner by adding a quiz to a Camtasia project. Each quiz can contain any or all of the following question types: Multiple choice, True/False, Fill in the blank, and Short answer.

Student Activity: Add a Quiz and a Question

1. Open **QuizMe.cmproj** from the **Camtasia3_MacData > Projects** folder.

2. Position the Playhead where you'd like the quiz to appear.

   ❑ on the **Timeline**, position the **Playhead** at end of the video (at **2:57;17**)

3. Insert a quiz.

   ❑ from the list of tools at the left, click **Interactivity**

   The Interactivity panel opens at the top left of the Editor.

   ❑ click **Add Quiz to Timeline**

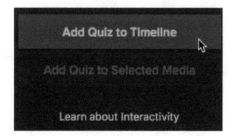

The new quiz is created at the Playhead's position with a default name, Quiz 1. Using the options on the Quiz properties (in the upper right of the Camtasia window), you can name the quiz, add questions, preview the quiz, and more.

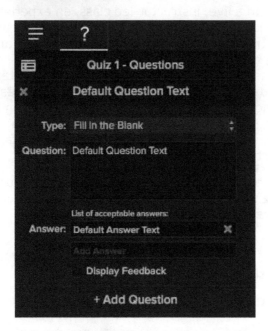

4. Rename the quiz.

   ☐ on the **Quiz Properties** panel, click **Quiz Option Properties**

   ☐ change the Quiz Name to **Folders Quiz**

5. Ensure that the quiz will score.

   ☐ from just above the **Preview** button, ensure that both **Viewer can see their results** and **Score quiz** are selected

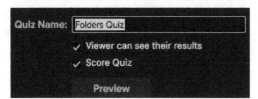

6. Specify the question type.

   ☐ on the **Quiz Properties** panel, click **Quiz Question Properties**

   ☐ from the **Type** drop-down menu, choose **Multiple Choice**

7. Edit the question.

   ☐ in the Question area, replace the placeholder text with **When giving a folder a name, how many characters can you use?**

8. Add four answers to the question.

   ☐ in the first Answer area, type **9**

   ☐ in the next Answer area, type **255**

   ☐ in the next Answer area, type **11**

   ☐ in the next Answer area, type **218**

   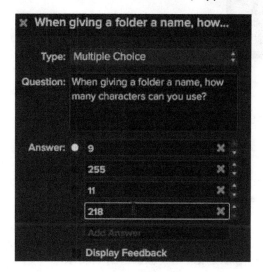

   Note: You'll always end up with an extra "Add answer..." placeholder (as shown in the image above). No worries. Unless you type something in that placeholder, the answer will not be part of the quiz.

9. Specify 255 as the correct answer.

   ☐ click the **circle** next to the second answer, **255**

Student Activity: Add a Fill in the Blank Question

1. Ensure that the **QuizMe** project is open.

2. Add a question.

   ❑ from the bottom of the Quiz properties panel, click **Add question**

   The new question appears below the first.

   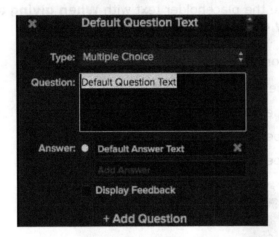

3. Specify the question type.

   ❑ from the **Type** drop-down menu, choose **Fill in the Blank**

4. Edit the question.

   ❑ replace the Question Text placeholder text with **The New Folder icon is found on the _____ tab of the Ribbon.**

5. Edit the Answer.

   ❑ in the **Answer** area, replace the placeholder text with **Home**

   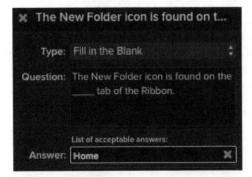

6. Save your work.

Quiz Confidence Check

1. Preview the quiz by clicking the **Preview** tool.

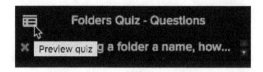

A preview of the quiz appears on the Canvas.

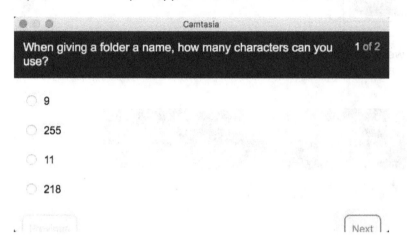

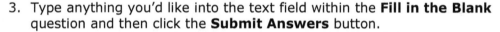

2. Select any of the answers in the first question and click the **Next** button.

3. Type anything you'd like into the text field within the **Fill in the Blank** question and then click the **Submit Answers** button.

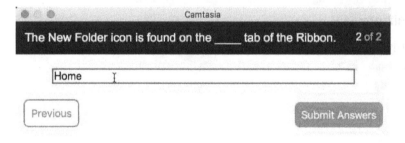

4. Click the **View Answers** button.

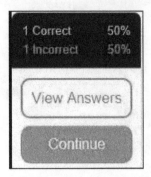

Correct answers are shown with a green check mark. Wrong answers are flagged with a red X.

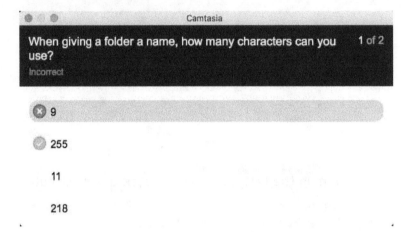

5. Close the Quiz preview.

6. Save the project.

Screencast.com

When you Share your Camtasia project, you can share it to YouTube, Vimeo, etc. However, if you Share the finished project locally, then what? How do your learners gain access to your content? If you have a Learning Management System or web server of your own, you can upload the rendered output files there. But what if you don't have either of those? Where can you upload your content so that it is readily available and, if it contains interactivity such as hotspots or a quiz, ensure that the interactivity works? Fortunately, TechSmith provides a free service called Screencast where you can test and share your content. The video you are about to work with contains a quiz. You'll upload the video to Screencast.com and be able to test the quiz.

> **Note:** You will need to create a free account on Screencast.com prior to starting the activity below. If you do not have an account, go to **www.screencast.com** and set one up now.

Student Activity: Share to Screencast.com

1. Open **ScreencastMe.cmproj** from the **Camtasia3_MacData > Projects** folder.

2. Produce and share a video on Screencast.com.

   ❏ choose **Share > Screencast.com**

   ❏ enter your Screencast.com email address and password

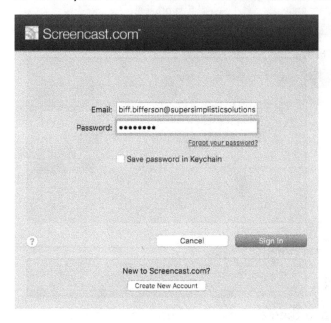

   ❏ click the **Sign In** button

   ❏ leave the Video title and folder as is

3. Set up the Quiz Reporting Options.

❑ from the bottom of the dialog box, ensure **Include Quiz** is selected

❑ click the **Options** button

The Quiz Settings dialog box opens.

❑ select **Report quiz results through email**

❑ in the Recipient email address and Confirm email address fields, type **your email address**

4. Require Viewer identity.

❑ from the **Viewer identity** area, select **Require viewers to input name & email address**

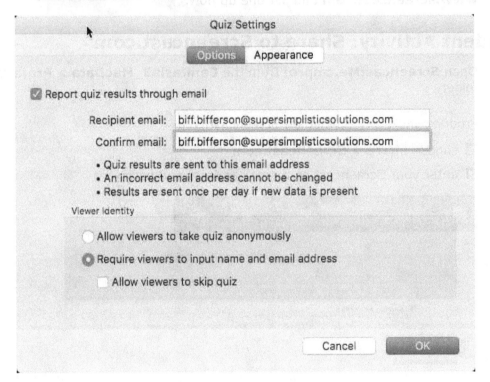

❑ click the **OK** button

You are returned to the Screencast.com screen.

❑ click the **Share** button

The lesson is exported and then automatically uploaded into your Screencast account.

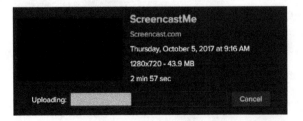

Screencast Confidence Check

1. On the Share History screen, click the **Visit** button to open the published lesson on Screencast.com. (If you already closed the Share History screen, you can reopen it at any time by choosing **Share > Share History**.

2. Start the video and you will be prompted to identify yourself (thanks to the **Viewer identity** option you selected a moment ago).

> ### A first name, last name, and email address are required to take this quiz.
>
> | Kevin |
> | Siegel |
> | ksiegel@iconlogic.com |
>
> ## Submit and View Quiz

3. Fill in the fields with your first name, last name, and email address.

4. Click the **Submit and View Quiz** button.

5. When the time comes to take the quiz, take it. You can answer the questions correctly or incorrectly.

6. After taking the quiz, continue through to the end of the video. When finished, close the browser.

7. If you have access to email, check you email. The quiz results should be sent to you from Camtasia Quiz Service.

   Note: The email comes from services@techsmith.com. If you don't see the email, you might want to check your SPAM folder and/or add TechSmith to your server's Safe/Allowed Senders List. Also, it was several hours before I received my first email from TechSmith.

The Quiz results include a summary containing the number of responses, the average score, the low score, and the high score. Specific details about the quiz results are included as CSV files that can be opened with Microsoft Excel or other spreadsheet applications. The CSV files contain details about who took the quiz, the questions they got right and wrong, etc.

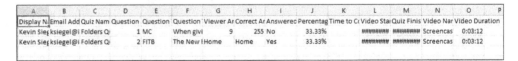

8. Close the e-mail.

9. Back in Camtasia, close any open dialog boxes/windows, save your work, and close the project.

iCONLOGiC
"Skills and Drills" Learning

Module 6: Markers, Hotspots, and Captions

In This Module You Will Learn About:

- Markers, page 104
- Hotspots, page 107
- Captions, page 109

And You Will Learn To:

- Add a Marker, page 104
- Add a Hotspot to the Timeline, page 107
- Create Closed Captions, page 109
- Control Caption Timing, page 113

Markers

Markers create navigation points within a video. When you add a table of contents to your finished lesson, the markers you add can be used to create hyperlinks (jumps) throughout the lesson. Allowing your learners to jump around the lesson is known as Branching.

Student Activity: Add a Marker

1. Open **MarkMe.cmproj** from the **Camtasia3_MacData > Projects** folder.

   Notice that there are new tracks in this project: Nav1, Nav2, and Nav3. These tracks contain simple shapes. Later, you will set things up so that learners will be able to click the shapes to access specific areas of the course (known as markers). You'll add the markers next.

2. Add a Marker.

   ❑ on the **Timeline**, drag the **Playhead** to beginning of the **Get Ready** group

   ❑ choose **Modify > Markers > Add Timeline Marker**

   A marker has been added above the Timeline. On the Properties panel, the new marker is ready to receive a name.

   ❑ on the **Properties** panel, change the **Maker name** to **Home**

Markers/TOC Confidence Check

1. Still working in the MarkMe project, move the Playhead to the beginning of the **Lesson 1** group.

2. Add a new marker (**Modify > Markers > Add Timeline Marker**) named **Lesson 1: Creating New Folders**.

3. Position the Playhead at the **Lesson 2** group.

4. Add a new marker named **Lesson 2: Renaming Folders**.

5. Position the Playhead at the **Lesson 3** group.

6. Add a new marker named **Lesson 3: Recycling and Restoring**.

   Your project should now contain four markers.

7. Share the project to **Screencast.com**.

8. Title the course **Working_with_Folders**.

9. Ensure **Create table of contents from markers** is selected.

10. Once the project is generated, view it on Screencast.com.

11. The Table of Contents can be opened via the icon on the playbar at the bottom of the lesson. If you click the icon, the TOC will open in the upper left of window. You can click any of the thumbnails to jump around the lesson.

12. Close the browser and return to Camtasia.

13. Close all open windows.

14. Save your work.

15. Close the project.

Hotspots

To maximize the effectiveness of your eLearning videos, you can add interactivity via a hotspot. The hotspots you add can allow your learners to jump to specific markers within a video, add links to websites, and more.

Here are the options available to you when you create a Hotspot:

Pause at end: Once clicked, the video stops based on the hotspot's end time on the Timeline.

URL: Takes the learner to a website.

Marker: Takes the learner to a specific Timeline marker.

Time: Takes the learner to a specific time in the video.

Student Activity: Add a Hotspot to the Timeline

1. Open **HotSpotMe.cmproj** from the **Camtasia3_MacData > Projects** folder.

   As mentioned at the beginning of this module, there are three shapes on the Canvas and at the beginning of the project (you can also see them on the Timeline in the **Nav1**, **Nav2**, and **Nav3** tracks). You are going to set it up so if learners click the shapes, they will jump to a specific part of the course. You already created the targets for those jumps when you added the **Home**, **Lesson 1**, **Lesson 2**, and **Lesson 3** markers earlier.

2. Add an Interactive Hotspot to an object on the Canvas.

   ☐ on the **Timeline**, **Nav1** track, double-click the green box containing the number **1**

   The object is displayed on the Canvas and selected.

   ☐ from the **Tools** panel at the left, click **Visual Effects**

   ☐ drag the **Interactive Hotspot** Visual Effect over to the **Canvas** and directly on top of the **green shape**

3. Add an Action to a Hotspot.

   ☐ with the hotspot on top of the shape selected, go to the **Properties** panel

   ☐ from the **Interactive Hotspot** area, ensure **Pause at end** is selected (this ensures that the video doesn't move forward without giving the learner a chance to click)

❑ select **Marker**

❑ from the Marker drop-down menu, choose **Lesson 1: Creating New Folders** (you learned how to create this particular marker on page 104)

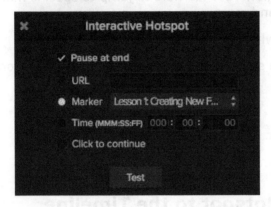

4. Save your work.

Hotspot Confidence Check

1. Add a second Interactive Hotspot and position it over the red shape of the group in the Nav2 track.

2. Make the target of the hotspot the **Lesson 2** marker.

3. Add a third and final Interactive Hotspot and position it over the shape in the Nav3 track.

4. Make the target of the hotspot the **Lesson 3** marker.

5. Share the project to **Screencast.com** with the Title **Working_with_Folders_Hotspots**.

6. Visit the lesson on Screencast.com and test any one of the hotspots.

7. When finished, close the browser and then return to Camtasia.

8. Save your work and close the project.

Captions

Adding Captions to a project, also known as closed captioning, allows you to provide descriptive information onscreen that matches the voiceover audio contained in your Camtasia project. Captions are helpful for learners who are not able to hear the audio component of a lesson.

There are a couple of ways you can add closed captions to a Camtasia project. The following lessons show you how to add the captions manually (by transcribing and copying/pasting).

Student Activity: Create Closed Captions

1. Open **CaptionMe.cmproj** from the **Camtasia3_MacData > Projects** folder.

    There are several audio clips in the Voiceover track. You're going to listen to some of the clips and manually create a few Captions.

2. Add captions manually.

    ❒ from the Tools panel, click **Audio Effects**

    ❒ from the list of Audio Effects, drag **Captions** on top of the first audio clip in the Voiceover Track

    The Caption Track opens just above the Timeline.

    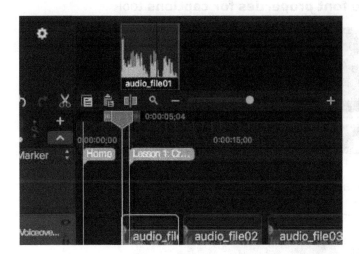

    ❒ on the **Caption Track**, click the **left side** of the audio waveform

    The first part of the audio plays and a typing area opens. In this first audio segment, the narrator says: "Welcome to Super Simplistic Solutions learning series. This is lesson one: Creating New Folders."

    ❒ type the following into the space beneath the background image:
    Welcome to Super Simplistic Solutions learning series.

The Caption you typed automatically appears on the Canvas. This is what a learner will see if they decide to use the lesson's closed captions.

3. Format the Caption text.

    ☐ on the **Caption Track**, click the left side of the audio waveform again

    ☐ click the **Change font properties for captions** tool

Font options appear at the top of the Canvas.

    ☐ change the font size to **18**

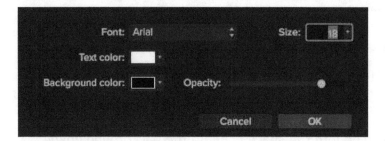

    ☐ click the **OK** button

On the Canvas, the change to the font size is immediate. And you are likely thinking to yourself that the smaller font size looks better than the clunky, larger font. However, keep in mind that the Captions aren't necessarily for you—they're for learners who cannot hear the audio. When creating eLearning content, you'll need to be on the alert to anything you might do in your project that does not conform to the Americans with Disabilities Act (ADA).

In case you're not familiar with ADA, it's a 1990 US civil rights law that prohibits discrimination against individuals with disabilities in all areas of public life, including jobs, schools, transportation, and all public and private places that are open to the general public. Generally speaking, the law exists to ensure that people with disabilities have the same rights and opportunities as everyone else and guarantees equal opportunity for individuals with disabilities in public accommodations, employment, transportation, state and local government services, and even eLearning.

In the case of font sizes used in Captions, a larger font is preferred because it is simply easier to see.

4. Restore the Caption's font size to its larger size.

   ❑ on the **Caption Track**, click the left side of the audio waveform again

   ❑ click the **Change font properties for captions** tool

   ❑ change the font size back to **32**

   ❑ click the **OK** button

5. Add another Caption.

   ❑ on the **Caption Track**, click the **right** side of the audio waveform

   ❑ type **This is lesson one: Creating New Folders.**

6. Preview the Captions.

☐ position the **Playhead** as far **left** as it can go

☐ on the **Canvas**, click the **Play** button to preview the lesson

This is lesson one: Creating New Folders.

Notice that the timing of the captions does not exactly match the voiceover audio (the first Caption is onscreen a bit too long). You'll fix that next.

Student Activity: Control Caption Timing

1. Ensure that the **CaptionMe.cmproj** project is open.

2. Adjust Caption Timing

   ❏ on the **Caption Track**, click the **left side** of the audio waveform

   ❏ from the bottom right of the caption screen, change the **Duration** to **3** seconds

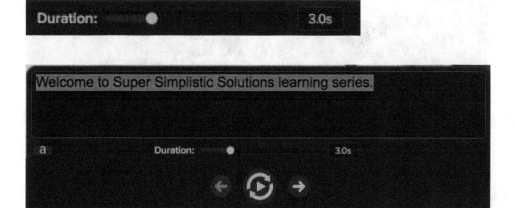

   ❏ on the Timeline, position the **Playhead** as far **left** as it can go

   ❏ on the **Canvas**, click the **Play** button to preview the lesson

   The Caption timing is more in sync with the voiceover audio.

Captions Confidence Check

1. Add a caption to the second audio file on the Timeline with the following text: **This lesson is going to teach you how to create a new folder on your computer,**

2. Share the project to Screencast.com. (Prior to clicking the Share button, choose **Closed captions** from the **Caption style** area.)

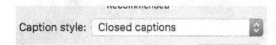

3. After the Export process is complete, Visit the page.

4. After starting the lesson, click the **CC** button on the playbar to view the Captions you added.

5. Close the browser window.

   Now you'll get a chance to copy and paste text from an existing voiceover script.

6. Hide Camtasia (to get it out of your way for a moment) and, from the **Camtasia3_MacData > Other_Assets** folder, open **CreatingFoldersVoiceoverScript**.

Audio File 1:
Welcome to Super Simplistic Solutions learning series.
This is lesson one: Creating New Folders.

Audio File 2:
This lesson is going to teach you how to create a new folder on your computer, how to rename it, and how to both delete and restore recycled items.

Audio File 3:
When creating folders keep in mind that you can create as many folders as you need.

---

7. In the **Audio File 2** text, select **"how to rename it, and how to both delete and restore recycled items"** and copy the text to the Clipboard.

8. Return to Camtasia and the CaptionMe project.

9. Still working in the section caption, click the right side of the waveform and paste the text you copied into the caption text area.

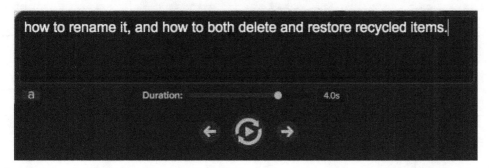

10. Save your work.

11. Close the project.

    And a hearty congratulations are in order... you have completed this book. You should now feel comfortable creating Camtasia projects from scratch, recording screen actions, and adding such Camtasia media and assets as videos, callouts, images, behaviors, audio, quizzes, and captions. You should also feel comfortable in your ability to Share your content locally, on YouTube, and on Screencast.com.

    I hope you enjoy using Camtasia to create eLearning as much as I do. Should you get stuck using Camtasia, the first place to look for help is online via the TechSmith Camtasia website (http://techsmith.com) and TechSmith blog (blogs.techsmith.com/category/tips-how-tos/). TechSmith has a great community offering free tips, tricks, and step-by-step videos. Feel free to reach out to me directly at **ksiegel@iconlogic.com**.

Notes

Index